FOR KING AND EMPIRE

THE CANADIANS IN THE SECOND BATTLE OF YPRES

April 22 to 26, 1915

© NORM CHRISTIE

For King and Empire
Volume: I
The Canadians at Ypres
April 1915

ISBN 0-9699039-3-6

Copyright 1996

Published by: Bunker to Bunker Books
34 Blue Spruce Cres.
Winnipeg, MB. R2M 4C2

Distributed by: C.E.F. Books   Bunker to Bunker Books
P.O. Box 29123   34 Blue Spruce Cres.
3500 Fallowfield Rd.   Winnipeg,
Nepean,   MB, R2M 4C2
ON K2J 4A9

Other Books in the Series

Front cover picture: The Brooding Soldier (Photo by S. Hickman)
Back cover picture: The posthumously-awarded medals of John Gloag of Winnipeg. Gloag was killed April 25th, 1915 in the Second Battle of Ypres. He was 20 years old.

Printed and bound by Hignell Printing Ltd., Winnipeg, MB. Canada

DEDICATION

This book is dedicated to
Private Randall Alexander Christie
8th Canadian Field Ambulance
1894–1972

and

Lieutenant John Christie, MC
Princess Patricia's Canadian Light Infantry
1892–1960

Was it so hard, Achilles,
So very hard to die?
Thou knowest and I know not —
So much the happier I

Patrick Shaw-Stewart, 1915

A Soldier of the First Contingent

TABLE OF CONTENTS

A unknown soldier of the 2nd Battalion killed at Ypres, April 1915.

INTRODUCTION TO THE YPRES BATTLEFIELD GUIDE

Thursday, April 22, 1915 was a beautiful spring day in Belgium. The thousands of Canadian volunteers who had rushed to join the colors in the autumn had easily weathered their first two months of an uneventful war in Europe. They'd learned the French routine. They'd dug and fortified defences. But by the end of that weekend 2,000 of them would be dead and Canada would have paid its first bill in the cause of King and Empire in the Great War.

Back in Canada, the first black-bordered letters and telegrams were received, briefly notifying mothers, fathers and wives that their sons and husbands were no more. The first casualty lists appeared in the newspapers, listing the killed, wounded and missing. The communities of this young country started to grasp the costs of the Great European War.

The Canadians' first battle won a strong reputation for the tenacious defence they offered. Through blind courage, they withstood the poisonous gas, the massive artillery bombardments and, although outnumbered, the frontal assaults of the German infantry.

This reputation for dependability was to continue throughout the later years of the war and gain the Canadians the reputation of the best fighting soldiers on the Western front.

By the end of the war, the cost to Canada, a country of seven million people, was over 60,000 dead and 220,000 wounded. More than 600,000 Canadians had enlisted. They had come from all walks of life and from the many ethnic groups which then populated Canada.

And it was in Flanders, at Ypres, Belgium, that their long road started.

Today the name of Ypres, St. Julien and Langemarck have little significance, but to our grandfathers and our fathers these names brought a certain pride and knowledge of those terrible days. As the last of the Great War veterans pass on, so does the legacy of their sacrifice and achievement. It has now become our heritage and our obligation to remember.

The objective of this book and of the series of books to follow is to remember *that* sacrifice and *our* heritage.

In many parts of France and Belgium the battlefields have not changed much. The trenches have gone, the bodies are buried in orderly cemeteries and only the occasional German blockhouse remains. But the small rural villages stand as they did in 1915, preserving for us the setting of the battles our forefathers witnessed in grimmer times.

As you travel through these battlefields and visit Ypres or Vimy you can gain some of that pride of being Canadian, that same pride felt by our grandfathers when they and their comrades paid the ultimate sacrifice with their blood.

GETTING THERE

Ypres or Ieper (as it is now called) is located in western Belgium, 20 kilometres north of the Belgian/French border. It is easily accessible from Paris (300 kilometres north) and Brussels (100 kilometres). From London, it is a two-hour drive to Dover, a 75-minute ferry ride to Calais, and a 45-minute drive from Calais. The opening of the Channel Tunnel has made a direct rail link from London to Lille, France, which is close to the Belgian border. Check with the Tourist Board for details. Rental cars are available in any of the above-mentioned cities and tourist offices can supply routes and details of hotels.

In Belgium, the main language is Flemish, an accented version of Dutch. About a third of Belgians speak French, which was the country's official language for centuries. However, as Flanders became richer and more industrialized and Flemish nationalism acquired more political clout, the Dutch language was accorded more and more official respect. In 1962, Brussels was made officially bilingual as a concession to the northerners. Belgians in general today speak several languages and English is widely understood.

There are approximately 21 Belgian francs (1996) to one Canadian dollar. In Ypres, French francs are also accepted in most stores and restaurants. Credit cards, such as VISA, Access or MasterCard are accepted, but please check with the hotel where you are staying. Always visit the Tourism Office to obtain information on accommodation or events of interest.

The following tour is based on staying in Ypres and departing from the Grote Markt or town square. However, if the Ypres battlefield tour is part of a larger itinerary, I recommend Arras, France, as another good base of operation. Although English is generally spoken in the main hotels of Arras, otherwise very little English is spoken. Brush up on your French before going.

In France, stores close between noon and 2:00 p.m. *always.* Be sure to obtain film and other necessities before closing! Stopping for a long lunch is a strict and revered tradition in continental Europe.

There are 3.5 French francs (1996) to one Canadian dollar.

Currency and traveler's checks can be exchanged at any bank.

WHAT TO BRING

Weather is very changeable in this part of Europe. Days can start sunny and change quickly to rain, hail or even a sprinkling of snow. Above all, be prepared for wet weather. For example, the average temperature in Belgium in July varies from 12 to 24°C.

Other than the obvious passport, traveler's checks and appropriate clothing, bring the following to ensure a successful trip:

- a bottle opener and cork screw

- binoculars

- a camera (with 100 and 200 ASA film)

- a compass

- rubber boots

- National Geographic Institute maps 1:25,000, numbers 28/1-2, 28/3-4 and 28/5-6 (these can be obtained at the Tourist Office in Ypres)

- Michelin map No. 51 (preferably the Commonwealth War Graves Commission overprint, showing all the cemeteries)

- reference books (do your research before departure)

ABOUT YPRES

Ypres (Ieper, Ypern) lies in the quiet, picturesque poppy fields of Flanders in western Belgium. Surrounded by hills, lakes and hop fields, this now-modern town has been one of Europe's strategic battlegrounds for centuries. Throughout its 1,000-year history, Ypres has always been a tempting prize and military strong point for its neighbors.

In the Middle Ages, the town was one of Belgium's jewels, the strength and wealth of Flanders. A centre of culture and commerce and a flourishing textile trade, Ypres was at its peak in the 13th century with a population of 40,000 with another 150,000 in the surrounding region.

It was at this time construction of the town's most famous building, the great Lakenhalle (Cloth Hall), a monument to Ypres's textile industry, was begun. Taking 100 years to build, this impressive covered market allowed ships to moor alongside to load and discharge cargoes onto a covered quay along the banks of the Yperlee. The Nieuwerck (Town Hall), now a tourist office, was completed some 300 years later. The upper storey, once used for storage, today houses two museums and a concert hall. From its 70-metre belfry, the hours are sounded by a 49-bell carillon.

Ypres' flourishing trade dropped significantly in 1383, when the town was attacked by troops from England and Ghent. Although Ypres resisted the siege, many weavers left, taking the livelihood of the town with them. By the 1500s, the population of the town was 5,000 and its importance had diminished.

Over the last 600 years, Ypres has been attacked by Spaniards, French, Austrians and Dutch. When Ypres became French in 1678, the city's defence works were revamped by renowned French military engineer Marshal Vauban. The six gates were reduced to four. These defences were able to withstand the wars of 1689-1712, but the end of the 18th century witnessed the rebuilding and dismantling of many of the town's defences. In 1815, prior to Waterloo, all exterior works were quickly reconstructed and defended by British troops. After Waterloo, when Belgium united with the Netherlands, Ypres again strongly fortified against any possible French invasion. In the 1830s, when

Belgium was granted independence, Ypres became Belgian and soon afterwards the Belgian government decided Ypres no longer needed to be fortified and levelled all the outer works. Walls and ramparts were removed to make room for railways and old gates demolished to allow wider passage on the roads.

The only gate left, still part of the original French walls, is the Lille Gate or Rijselsepoort at the southern extreme of town. Where the Menin Gate stands today on the town's eastern flank, in memory of the missing of the First World War, once was graced by the town's most beautiful gate. The Antwerp Gate was refashioned into the Corne d'Anveers by Vauban and named after Napoleon when he visited Ypres in 1804 and an imperial eagle carved into the stonework.

In 1914, Ypres once again lay in the path of warring nations. The German cavalry rode into the town on October 13. The Burgomaster was held to ransom for 75,000 Bfr, but the British Expeditionary Force reached the town the next day and occupied it entirely. The great artillery barrage which began on November 22 damaged ancient buildings and set the Cloth Hall on fire. Civilians suffered considerably and were finally evacuated on May 9, 1915 during the Second Battle of Ypres, when the Cloth Hall, Collegiate Church of St. Martin and other important buildings were destroyed. Although many returned to the ruins of their homes during the comparative quiet of 1916, Ypres was essentially in military hands until the Third Battle of Ypres in 1917. In the spring of 1918, Ypres was nearly lost to the Germans, but the British lines held and the final Allied advance relieved the town, ousting the last German troops September 28.

Belgium was again a trampling ground for occupying German forces in the Second World War. Damage from both wars was so catastrophic that much of the country had to be rebuilt from scratch. Ypres was built from the bottom up after the First World War.

Prominent in Ypres today are its refashioned St. Martin's Cathedral, the towering Cloth Hall and reconstructed 17th century façades along many streets. The Grote Markt (Great Market) is the town centre and is surrounded by the Courthouse, the old Town Hall, the Kasselrijgebouw (with seven deadly sins carved on

Ruins of the Cloth Hall, July 1916
(PUBLIC ARCHIVES OF CANADA PA314)

its façade) and numerous cafés and restaurants where you can enjoy a beer, a coffee or a good lunch. Market day is Saturday morning.

Prices for food and accommodation in Belgium are generally steep. There are good relais (inns) in the countryside where you can spend the night and have lunch or dinner. Book ahead for a room in a hotel or a relais and make reservations for meals. The tourist office is in the Cloth Hall (tel. 57 200724) and offers comprehensive tourist information in English, as well as guidebooks, maps and leaflets listing hotels and restaurants.

Here is a list of hotels, restaurants, museums and special events to get you started:

Four-star hotels include *Hotel Ariane,* Slachthuisstraat 58 (near Grote Markt), 8900 Ieper, tel. 57 218218; *Hotel Rabbit,* Industrielaan 19, 8900 Ieper, tel. 57 217000; *Regina Hotel,* Grote Markt 45, 8900 Ieper, tel. 57 218888.

Some three-star hotels are *Kasteelhof 't Hooghe,* Meenseweg 481, 8092 Ieper, tel. 57 468787; *Hotel Sultan,* Grote Markt 33, 8900 Ieper, tel. 57 219030.

Some restaurants to consider are *Hostellerie St. Nicolas,* G. de Stuersstraat 6 (near Grote Markt), 8900 Ieper, tel. 57 200622 (some rooms available also); *Gasthof't Zweerd,* Grote Markt 2, 8900 Ieper, tel. 57 200475 (some rooms); *Restaurant Den Anker,* Grote Markt 30, 8900 Ieper,tel. 57 200528 (brasserie/tearoom/restaurant); *'t Hooge,* Meenseweg 467, 8902 Ieper, tel. 57 468446 (this is a café housed in a rebuilt school next to the Hooge Crater Museum); *Restaurant De Palingbeek,* Palingbeekstraat 18, 8902 Ieper, tel. 57 205672; *Restaurant De Steenen Haan,* Komenseweg 21, 8902 Ieper, tel. 57 205486; *De Wijngaard,* Mk. Fochlaan 8, 8900 Ieper, tel. 57 204230 (restaurant/steakhouse); *Zillebekevijver,* Zillebekevijverdreef 2, 8902 Zillebeke, tel. 57 200086 (tavern/tea room).

You might want to check out some of the following museums. Note, most museums are open from 9:30 a.m. to noon and 1:30 to 5:30 p.m. and closed on Mondays, but check with the individual museum; *Educational Museum,* Cloth Hall, Grote Markt, 8900 Ieper, tel. 57 200724, open April 1–October 31; *Remembrance Museum "Ypres Salient '14-18",* Cloth Hall, Grote Markt, 8900 Ieper, tel. 57 200724, open April 1–November 15; *Museum Merghelynck,* A. Merghelynckstraat 2, 8900 Ieper, tel. 57 203042, open April 1–October 30; *Belle Museum,* Rijselsestraat 38, 8900 Ieper, tel. 57 204831, open April 1–October 30; *Stedelijk (Municipal) Museum,* Ieperleestraat 31, 8900 Ieper, tel. 57 218300, open April 1–October 30; *Hooge Crater 14–18 Museum,* Meenseweg 467, 8902 Zillebake, tel. 57 468446, open April 1 –November 31; *Hill 60-Queen Victoria Rifles Museum,* Zwarteleenstraat 40, 8902 Zillebeke, tel. 57 206276; *62-Sanctuary Wood Museum,* Canadalaan 26, 8902 Zillebeke, tel. 57 466373.

The principal event of the year in Ypres is Kattenwoensdag or the Cat Festival, which takes place on the second Sunday of May. Based on the mediaeval belief that evil spirits adopted the physical form of a cat, cats were widely persecuted and killed. Today, plush toy cats are thrown from the belfry by the festival jester. Until 1817, live cats were thrown.

Every three years, a Parade of Cats honors the animal as portrayed in literature and folklore (next parade 1997). Thousands of costumed revelers take part in the festival.

This guide uses place names of the 1914–18 period. Below is a list of place names as you will see them today (on the left) and as they were known during the war (on the right).

New	Old
Sint-Jan	St. Jean
Ieper	Ypres
Poelkapelle	Poelcapelle
Fortuinhoek	Fortuin
Roeselare	Roulers
Wieltje	Wieltje
Sint-Juliaan	St. Julien
Kerselaar	Keerselaere
Langemark	Langemarck
Pilkem	Pilckem
's-Graventafel	Gravenstafel
Passendale	Passchendaele
Zonnebeke	Zonnebeke
Frezenberg	Frezenberg
Westhoek	Westhoek
Poperinge	Poperinghe

A DIVISION.

(B. W.E., Pt. VII., New Armies, 1915.)

	Officers	Other Ranks	Total	Carts	Wagons
Headquarters.............	22	98	120	1	1
Infantry (48 Machine Guns)	384	12,015	12,399	48	189
Pioneer Battalion.........	30	1,008	1,038	4	22
H.-Q. Divisional Artillery.	4	19	23	1 Motor Car	
Field Artillery, 48 18-pr. guns...................	72	2,190	2,262	33	195
Field Artillery, Howitzer Brigade, 16 4.5″ guns..	23	688	711	11	50
Divisional Ammunition Column	12	540	552	3	96
H.-Q. Divisional Engineers	3	10	13	1	—
3 Field Companies, Royal Engineers.............	18	675	693	27	30
1 Signal Company	6	204	210	1	14
Cavalry Squadron.........	6	154	160	—	3
Cyclists	8	196	204	1	1
Motor Machine Gun Battery, 6 m.g.........	4	55	59	5 Cars, 27 Motorcycles	
Divisional Train (A.S.C.)..	25	482	507	5	204
3 Field Ambulances (A.M.C.)...............	30	714	744	12	39
Sanitary Section (A.M.C.)	1	27	28	—	—
Workshop (A.S.C.)	1	20	21	1 Motor Car 3 Lorries	
Mobile Veterinary Section	1	27	28	—	2
	650	19,122	19,772	147	846

An Infantry A Division, 1915

COMPONENTS OF THE
1ST CANADIAN INFANTRY DIVISION
YPRES 1915

1st Infantry Brigade	2nd Infantry Brigade	3rd Infantry Brigade
1st Battalion (Western Ontario)	5th Battalion (Saskatchewan)	13th Battalion (Black Watch of Montreal)
2nd Battalion (Eastern Ontario)	7th Battalion (British Columbia)	14th Battalion (Royal Montreal Regiment)
3rd Battalion (Toronto Regiment)	8th Battalion (90th Rifles of Winnipeg)	15th Battalion (48th Highlanders of Toronto)
4th Battalion (Central Ontario)	10th Battalion (Alberta)	16th Battalion (Canadian Scottish)

1st Division Cavalry: 19th Alberta Dragoons
1st Canadian Division Cyclist Corps
1st Divisional Signals Company
1, 2, and 3 Field Companies Canadian Engineers
1, 2, and 3 Canadian Field Ambulances
1, 2, and 3 Brigades Canadian Field Artillery

WAR ESTABLISHMENT OF AN INFANTRY BATTALION
FOR OVERSEAS SERVICE, 1915-16.

Headquarters.	C.E.F.	B.E.F.	Machine Gun Section.	C.E.F.	B.E.F.
Lieut-Colonel..........	1	1	Subaltern...............	1	1
Major.................	2	1	Sergeants..............	2	2
Adjutant..............	1	1	Corporals..............	1	1
Assistant Adjutant.....	1	0	Privates...............	21	21
Quarter-Master........	1	1	Drivers, 1st line Tpt....	6	6
Signalling Officer.......	1	0	Batmen[2]...............	1	1
Sergeant Major........	1	1			
Quarter-Master Sergt..	1	1	Total......	35	35
Orderly Room Clerks[1].	1	2			
Sergeant Drummer....	1	0	Company.		
Sergeant Cook.........	1	1			
Transport Sergeant....	1	1	Major (or Capt.)........	1	1
Sergeant Shoemaker...	1	1	Capt. (2nd in Command)	1	1
Drivers, Transport.....	9	10	Subalterns.............	4	4
Drivers, spare animals.	2	2	Com. Sergt.-Major......	1	1
Batmen[2]...............	10	6	Com. Q.-M. Sergeant...	1	1
			Sergeants..............	8	8
Pioneers.			Drummers or Buglers..	4	0
			Corporals..............	10	10
Pioneer Sergeant......	1	1	Privates...............	188	192
Pioneers	10	10	Drivers, 1st line Tpt....	3	3
			Batmen[2]...............	6	6
Signallers.					
			Total......	227	227
Sergeant...............	1	1			
Corporal...............	1	1	Base Details.		
Privates[3]..............	15	15			
			Sergt. of the Band.....	1	0
Stretcher Bearers......	16	16	Sergeant Master Tailor	1	0
Orderlies for M.O.[4].....	2	2	Bandsmen..............	19	0
			Storemen[5].............	4	0
Total......	81	74	First reinforcement....	94	0
Attached.			Total......	119	0
Paymaster.............	1	0	Summary.		
Medical Officer.........	1	1			
R.A.M.C. for water duty			Headquarters with		
Corporal.........	1	1	attached..............	89	82
Privates..........	4	4	Machine Gun Section.	35	35
Armourer	1	1	Companies[5] (4 of 227)....	908	908
Interpreter.............	0	1	Base Details...........	119	0
Total......	89	82	Total......	1151	1025

[1] Orderly Room Clerk may be a sergeant or a corporal.

[2] Batmen are fully armed and trained soldiers and are available for duty in the ranks.

[3] Seven (7) may be lance corporals.

[4] One of the M.O.'s orderlies may be a sergeant (Medical Sergt.) and the other a lance corporal. The latter drives the cart for medical equipment.

[5] One storeman will mobilize with each company.

THE SECOND BATTLE OF YPRES
April and May 1916

The Men Who Served

When Britain declared war in August 1914, all British dominions and colonies were automatically at war. This included Canada. Canada's immediate offer to Britain of a contingent of 25,000 men was accepted and Canada began to mobilize. Those first volunteers, all members of the 1st Canadian Division, were the ones to face the gas at Ypres.

Before 1914, Canada had a large militia force comprising men who joined the local militia, often for social, political or commercial reasons. Being a member of the far-ranging militia was socially desirable and always improved the sociability of a man-about-town, whether in Edmonton or Montreal. If the unit was associated with a famous British regiment, then all the better. A kilted regiment was the best. These were the men, officered by politicians or businessmen, who came together in September 1914.

By far, the majority of men were immigrants and reflected the mass immigration to Canada from the British Isles between 1880 and 1914.

A breakdown of this original contingent shows 30 per cent of them were born in Canada and 60 per cent were from Britain. The U.S.A. provided another 2.5 per cent. The officers were predominantly Canadian. These statistics reveal the many recent immigrants jumping at the opportunity to return home, whether for patriotic or personal reasons. Western Canada, the home of many of the new immigrants, provided a disproportionate number of enlistees.

The prospect of adventure, a change in a mundane life and just "doing the right thing" were major motivations for these early volunteers. Many had served in the Boer War and they had all been raised on the adventurous stories of the British Empire. All this contributed to their enthusiasm. Few anticipated the war would endure or be as bloody as it was and there were some initial problems. More than 5,000 men were discharged before they left the country. Some 2,200 were declared medically unfit. Another 377 were discharged due to a protest by an unhappy wife or parent and 282 requested their own discharge.

In October 1914, what was to become the 1st Canadian Division sailed for Britain. Whether from the Queen's Own Rifles of Canada (Toronto), the Calgary Rifles or the Royal Highlanders of Canada (Montreal), these men were about to face an experience from which few would emerge unscathed.

Historical Overview

By April 1915, the defence around Ypres had been established. The Race to the Sea and the First Battle of Ypres (October and November 1914) had left a semicircular area east of Ypres in French, British and Belgian hands. The precarious nature of this bulge was a clear advantage for the Germans who held most of the high positions on the ridge east of Ypres.

After their offensive of 1914, the Germans had decided to focus on eliminating the Russians on the Eastern Front. Nevertheless, at Ypres they saw an opportunity to burst the Allied bubble that was the Ypres Salient, complete the capture of Belgium and perhaps trap the Allied forces inside the salient. To assist this attack they planned to use a new, secret weapon, CHLORINE GAS. Intelligence reports indicating the Germans were about to attack with gas were ignored.

The Canadians arrived in France at the end of February 1915 and entered the line near Armentières. They suffered their first casualties there from snipers, but otherwise they remained untouched by battle. They were moved to the northeastern portion of the salient in mid-April to relieve French troops. The men were astounded by the poor defensive works they had inherited and immediately set to work to improve their positions.

By April 22, the men of the 1st Canadian Division were established in a line that ran from 50 metres north of the Ypres-Poelcappelle road to the Gravenstafel-Passchendaele road. In the line, respectively from south to north, were the 5th (Saskatchewan) and 8th (90th Rifles of Winnipeg) Battalions of the 2nd Canadian Infantry Brigade and the 15th (48th Highlanders of Toronto) and 13th (Black Watch of Montreal) Battalions of the

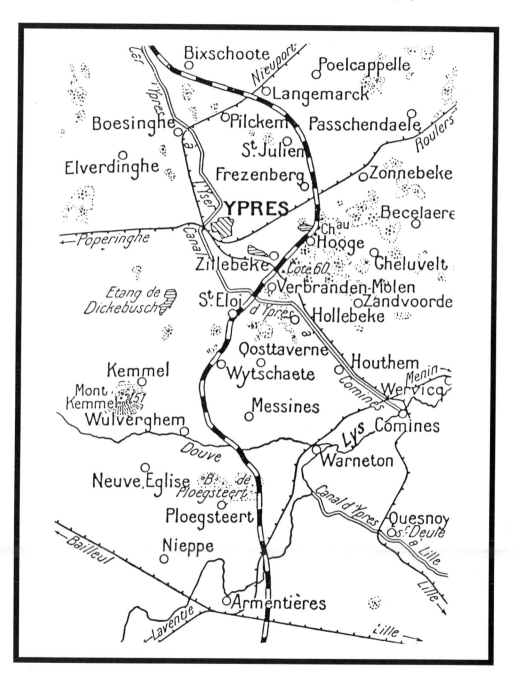

The Front Lines Prior to the Battle

3rd Brigade. The 7th (British Columbia) and 14th (Royal Mounted Regiment) Battalions were in close support of the battalions in the front line. Activity all along the front line was normal.

At 5 p.m. a large cloud of what turned out to be poison gas was observed rolling toward the French positions north of the 13th Battalion. In a short period the French colonial troops, suffering severely from the physical and psychological effects of the gas, broke and fled toward Ypres. They left a wide-open northern flank from the immediate left of the Canadians as far as the Ypres Canal. Within an hour, the German infantry was pouring into the gap. The situation was critical.

The Canadian commanders in the field were inexperienced in battle and had no idea how to cope with the gas but, to their credit, they did not panic.

Men of the 13th Battalion were ordered to form a protective flank just north of the Ypres-Poelcappelle road, extending toward St. Julien. With the remnants of the French troops, they poured on flanking fire and prevented the Germans from advancing freely behind the Canadians. Undoubtedly this heroic action, which cost so many lives, was the decisive point in the battle.

The Germans were surprised by the success of the gas and now had fire to contend with from the Canadian flank. They seemed reluctant to advance and were unable to effectively exploit the opportunity provided by the gas.

At nightfall the Canadians, although exposed to the Germans, were able to reassess their position and over the next four chaotic days fight to close the open flank in a series of piecemeal attacks and withdrawals.

During the evening of April 22, the 10th (Alberta) and 16th (Canadian Scottish) Battalions were ordered forward to attack a position taken by the Germans at Kitchener's Wood west of the village of St. Julien and to secure the line from the wood to the positions along the Ypres-Poelcappelle road.

At midnight, in pitch darkness, the inexperienced troops attacked in a tight formation against unknown German positions. They charged the wood and succeeded in driving out the

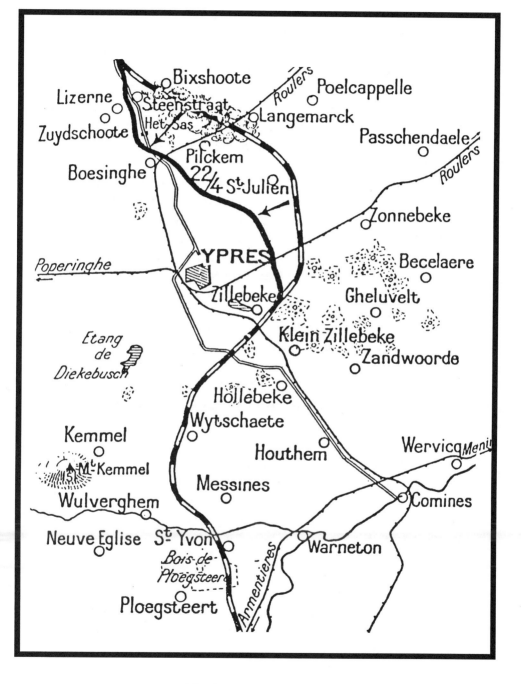

The Attack, April 22, 1915

Germans but took heavy losses, including the commander of the 10th Battalion, Lieutenant Colonel Russell Boyle.

By morning, it was evident the positions were untenable and the survivors were forced to withdraw to a position south of the wood. They had handed the Germans a setback but the result of poor planning and sending in inexperienced troops was sadly illustrated in the decimated ranks of the two battalions. However, at least another portion of the open flank had been closed.

On April 23, more Canadian troops were forced into the foray. The 2nd (Eastern Ontario) and 3rd (Toronto Regiment) Battalions reinforced the remnants of the 16th and 10th south of Kitcheners Wood and joined the 14th Battalion holding the village of St. Julien. The Canadians and British troops were ordered to secure the flank closer to Ypres. The objective of the 1st (Western Ontario) and 4th (Central Ontario) Battalions (which had been in reserve west of Ypres) was to recapture the east-west ridge south of Pilckem village, Mauser Ridge.

The Germans were clearly seen preparing their positions on the ridge and yet, at 5:25 a.m., in broad daylight, across an open field, against an entrenched position, the Canadians attacked. The result was predictable. Within minutes the battalions were forced to the ground to save their lives. Many were unable to do so.

At 2:45 p.m., in conjunction with a major British attack, they again attempted to capture the ridge. Their position advanced against the Germans and closed the open flank. Still their security was tenuous and they had suffered heavy losses, including the death of the commander of the 4th Battalion, Lieutenant Colonel Birchall.

At the apex of the salient, April 23 was a quiet day for the Canadians but on April 24, the Germans released gas against the 15th and 8th Battalions. The main force of the gas attack was south of the Ypres-Poelcappelle road. The 15th was overwhelmed and their line gave way. Their collapse was disastrous for the Canadians in St. Julien.

Cecil Mack Merritt.

MERRITT, CECIL MACK, Capt., 16th Battn. (Canadian Scottish, 72nd Seaforth Highlanders), Canadian Expeditionary Force, last surviving *s.* of Lieut.-Col, William Ingersoll Merritt, of 6, Sumner Place, South Kensington, London, late 30th (East Lancashire) and 4th Manchester Regts., by his wife, Mary Beatrice, 3rd dau. of Major-Gen. Frank Adams, C.B., and granddau. of Henry Cadwallader Adams, of Anstey Hall, co. Warwick, J.P., D.L. ; *b.* St. Catharine's, Ontario, Canada, 6 Jan. 1877 ; educ. St. Paul's School, London ; went to Canada in 1895, and joined the Royal Grenadier (Militia) Regt. in 1896. He was one of the few who went into Dawson in the rush of '98 over the Edmonton trail, the journey taking him two years. After leaving the Yukon he returned to England and was for a short time on the London Stock Exchange. He went to Vancouver in 1904, and when the 72nd Regt. Seaforth Highlanders of Canada was formed in Nov. 1910, he was appointed one of its senior Capts. He received his Majority in that Regt. 13 Oct. 1914. He was on Major-Gen. Sir Sam Hughes's Staff during his visit to the Imperial Army manœuvres in 1912, and on the outbreak of war at once volunteered for Imperial service, and was given command of a coy. in the 16th Battn. " Canadian Scottish," 1st Canadian Division. He went with them to France in Feb. 1915, and was present at the Battle of Neuve Chapelle. On 22 April, 1915, during the Second Battle of Ypres he was leading his coy. in the charge made by the Canadian Scottish near St. Julien, to check the first rush of the Germans after their gas attack, when he was wounded in the leg. He refused to leave his men, and with them occupied the German trenches. Next morning he was killed while encouraging his men during a counter-attack. He was mentioned in F.M. Sir John (now Lord) French's Despatch of 31 May, 1915, for gallant and distinguished service in the field. His commanding officer, Col. R. E. Edwards Leckey, wrote : " Cecil Merritt was one of the finest officers I ever knew. . . . He was wounded in the charge, but not severely, and still continued to lead his men on. He remained in the trenches we had captured, and when a counter-attack was threatened he got up to shoot over the parapet with his revolver. It was then he received his fatal wound. No one could have been braver and no one could have led his men better than he did. His name has been submitted for the Military Cross " ; and brother officers speak of his " personal bravery and spirit of dash and tenacity," and of the admiration which his men had for him ; and a Private wrote : " He was wounded twice but would not expose his men to be carried back to the dressing station, and after some hours in the captured trenches heard there was a counter-charge from the Germans, and it was then he received the fatal shot in his head." At St. Paul's he took a leading part in the school life, being captain of the football XV. He was one of the first captains of the well-known Harlequin Rugby Football Club. He *m.* at Vancouver, B.C., 4 Dec. 1905, Sophie Almon, eldest dau. of the Hon. Sir Charles Hibbert Tupper, K.C.M.G., and had two sons and a dau. : Charles Cecil Ingersoll, *b.* 10 Nov. 1908 ; Francis William, *b.* 16 Aug. 1913 ; and Beatrice Ormonde, *b.* 14 Feb. 1907.

Meritt was one of nine officers of the 16th Battalion who died at Ypres. The graves of seven were never found or identified.

Like many officers of the 1st Contingent, Merritt led a successful business life and was well-connected. His father-in-law was Sir Charles Hibbert Tupper, son of the former Canadian Prime Minister Charles Tupper. His brother-in-law, Victor Gordon Tupper, was killed in 1916.

Merritt left a wife and three children. His eldest son, Charles Cecil Ingersoll Merritt, won the Victoria Cross with the South Saskatchewan Regiment at Dieppe August 19, 1942.

From the Roll of Honour

BIRCHALL, ARTHUR PERCIVAL DEARMAN, Lieut.-Col. Commanding 4th Battn. Canadian Expeditionary Force, and Capt. Royal Fusiliers, 2nd *s.* of the late J.... Dearman Birchall, of Bowden Hall, co. Gloucester, by his wife, Emily, dau. of John Towitt, of Harehills, Leeds ;

Arthur P. D. Birchall.

b. Bowden Hall, 7 March, 1877, and was educ. at Eton and Magdalen College, Oxford. He obtained a University Commission, being gazetted 2nd Lieut. to the Royal Fusiliers (City of London Regt.), 23 May, 1900, and was promoted Lieut. 11 April, 1902, Capt. 1 Oct. 1908, Major, and Lieut.-Col. 22 Sept. 1914. From 25 March, 1904, to 24 March, 1907, he was Adjutant of the Royal Fusiliers, and on 15 April, 1910, was seconded for service with the Royal Canadian Regiment, and later he was on the Instructional Staff, Western Canada. In Aug. 1914, he was invalided home from Canada, but recovered sufficiently to rejoin the 1st Canadian Contingent in Nov., and acted as Staff Capt. to the 1st Brigade. Always popular and a keen and most efficient officer he was appointed to the colonelcy of the 4th Canadians in February, and was killed in action in the attack on the Pilkem Ridge, near Ypres, 23 April, 1915 ; *unm.* Speaking of this action F.M. Sir John French said : " The Canadians had many casualties, but their gallantry and determination undoubtedly saved the situation. Their conduct has been magnificent throughout" ; and the Official Report from the Canadian Record Officer at the Front was as follows : " The fighting continued without intermission all through the night, and to those who observed the indications that the attack was being pushed with ever-growing strength, it hardly seemed possible that the Canadians, fighting in positions so difficult to defend, and so little the subject of deliberate choice, could maintain their resistance for any long period. At 6 a.m. on Friday (April 23) it became apparent that the left was becoming more and more involved, and a powerful German attempt to outflank it developed rapidly. The consequences, if it had been broken or outflanked, need not be insisted upon. They were not merely local. It was therefore decided, formidable as the attempt undoubtedly was, to try and give relief by a counter-attack upon the first line of German trenches, now far, far advanced from those originally occupied by the French. This was carried out by the Ontario 1st and 4th Battns. of the 1st Brigade, under Brig.-Gen. Mercer, acting in combination with a British brigade. It is safe to say that the youngest private in the ranks, as he set his teeth for the advance, knew the task in front of him, and the youngest subaltern knew that all rested upon its success. It did not seem that any human being could live in the shower of shot and shell which began to play upon the advancing troops. They suffered terrible casualties. For a short time every other man seemed to fall, but the attack was pressed ever closer and closer. The 4th Canadian Battn. at one moment came under a particularly withering fire. For a moment—not more—it wavered. Its most gallant commanding officer, Lieut.-Col. Birchall, carrying, after an old fashion, a light cane, coolly and cheerfully rallied his men, and, at the very moment when his example had infected them, fell dead at the head of his battn. With a hoarse cry of anger they sprang forward (for, indeed, they loved him) as if to avenge his death. The astonishing attack which followed, pushed home in direct frontal fire made in broad daylight, by battns. whose names should live for ever in the memories of soldiers, was carried to the first line of German trenches. After a hand-to-hand struggle the last German who resisted was bayoneted, and the trench was won. The measure of this success may be taken when it is pointed out that this trench represented in the German advance the apex in the breach which the enemy had made in the original line of the Allies, and that it was 2½ miles south of that line. This charge, made by men who looked death indifferently in the face—for no man who took part in it could think that he was likely to live—saved, and that was much, the Canadian left. But it did more. Up to the point where the assailants conquered or died, it secured and maintained during the most critical moment of all the integrity of the Allied line. For the trench was not only taken, it was held thereafter against all comers, and in the teeth of every conceivable projectile, until the night of Sunday, the 25th, when all that remained of the war-broken, yet victorious battns. was relieved by fresh troops." Major R. Hayter, Brigade-Major, 1st Canadian Brigade wrote : " Your brother, Percy, fell on the 23rd, leading his battn. in the first Canadian counter-attack on the 23rd made by the French, British, and 1st and 4th Canadian battns., just east of the Ypres Canal. His battn. lost all its officers but four, and some 560 casualties other ranks, but they never wavered and got into the enemy's line, saved the day, and prevented the enemy's advance south along the east bank of the canal. We are still being desperately engaged, and I cannot write much, but I am sure you will be glad to hear that he has been recommended for the Victoria Cross. He was wounded, had his wound dressed, was wounded again, yet would go on, and fell, leading the charge which took the trenches. . . . I had a written message from him timed 4.20 p.m. acknowledging an order, and I hope some day to be able to give it to you. His loss has been the greatest blow the contingent could have had. Loved by all, and worshipped by his officers and men, we feel that it was his personal magnetism alone which kept his regt. together, and enabled them to hold what they had gained. All our deepest sympathies are with you and your family, but his end could not have been more glorious " ; and the following tribute from an old friend appeared in " The Times " (29 April, 1915) : " The claim to have been the most popular officer in the Army is a large one, and may be advanced in the name of many a candidate. But it is probable that all who in any true sense had made Birchall's acquaintance will claim that no officer could have been more deeply, and probably none more widely, beloved and admired. At Eton, at Magdalen, and for fifteen years in the Army, he was for ever winning to himself friends by the simple but irresistible charm of his nature—by his manliness and sportsmanship, his humour and high spirits, his enthusiasm for his profession in general for the better things of life. Joining the newly-formed 4th Battn. of the Royal Fusiliers during the South African War, as a university candidate, he became closely identified with its fortunes for some ten years; and he was largely responsible for raising it to the high level of the older battns. of that famous regt. Beloved alike by his brother officers and men, he was equally prominent as a leader in soldiering and in sport : in the field of manœuvre as in the football, the hockey, the hunting, but especially the cricket field he always played a fine sporting game. After ably fulfilling the second adjutancy of his battn., he received the singular distinction of being selected— one of two officers from the whole Army—to be attached to the Canadian Forces, according to a scheme for the mutual benefit of both services. In Canada, he inevitably won through to the same affectionate and admiring popularity as at home. His period of appointment was extended, he was appointed to the Staff, and was given an almost transcontinental district of supervision. The characteristic energy which he threw into this work in the unaccustomed climate caused a temporary breakdown in his health, and bitter was his grief, on returning to England, shortly before the outbreak of war, to find himself entirely forbidden on medical grounds to take for the present the share in active service for which he had keenly prepared and eminently fitted himself. To such advantage, however, did he make use of his time, even of sickness, that, in the intervals of being visited by a constant stream of devoted friends from two continents, he compiled the admirable little manual for the use of regimental officers in the present emergency training, which he entitled " Rapid Training of a Company for War " (Gale & Polden, Aldershot). This book rapidly attained a wide success, and was brought up to date in a second (and subsequent) edition, just as he himself, recently promoted Major, was appointed first a Staff Captain in the Canadian Expeditionary Force, and in immediate succession given command of the 4th Canadian Infantry a few days before it sailed for the front." Col. Birchall resided at Saintbridge House, Gloucester. His brother, Capt. J. Dearman Birchall is (1916) serving with the Royal Gloucestershire's Hussars Yeomanry.

From the Roll of Honour

With the apex of the Canadian position broken, the Germans stormed through the gap, attacking St. Julien and Fortuin to the south and the Canadian positions on the Gravenstafel Ridge to the east. Surrounded by the Germans, St. Julien was captured and, with it, many men of the 14th, 2nd and 3rd Canadian Battalions who had been trapped by the collapse of the apex. To the east, the fighting at the foot of the Gravenstafel Ridge was fierce and only through the magnificent courage of the 7th Battalion (brought in to hold the position) were the Germans slowed. Their bravery, however, bore heavy costs — 176 men killed and 267 captured.

By the end of the day, half the Gravenstafel Ridge including the Canadian strongpoint of Locality "C" had fallen. St. Julien had fallen. Seven of the 12 Canadian battalions in the field had been decimated. Fifteen hundred Canadians were prisoners (the largest number of Canadian prisoners taken in the war)[1].

The 8th and 5th Battalions, which were surprisingly still in the position they occupied on April 21, came under attack by the Germans on April 25. They were eventually forced to make a fighting retreat to the Gravenstafel Ridge.

The following day, the Canadians were relieved and, although they remained in the salient, were not again involved in the heavy fighting. Over the following days, British and Indian troops attempted to recapture the lost position. Sadly, their attacks took place in daylight across open fields and the Germans made them pay. Their attack to retake St. Julien on April 25 was no more successful than the Canadian attacks at Kitcheners Wood and Mauser Ridge. Losses were great and gains were negligible.

On April 26 and 27, Indian troops tried to recapture Mauser Ridge, but their advance was unsuccessful in dislodging the Germans and losses were heavy.

On May 4, the British evacuated the further extremities of the Ypres Salient and obtained a better line of defence. As part of the general withdrawal on May 3 and 4, the 27th Imperial Division

---

[1] Only at Hong Kong in 1941 and Dieppe in 1942 were more Canadians captured.

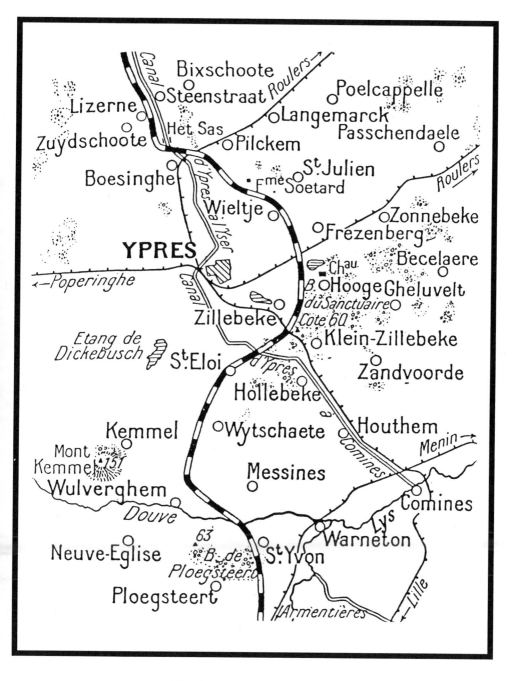

The Front Lines After the Battle

moved back from Zonnebeke to a position north of the Ypres-Menin road, east of Hooge and roughly five kilometres south of the Canadian positions.

A Canadian battalion, the Princess Patricia's Canadian Light Infantry (PPCLI), was a member of the 27th Division and was, in fact, the only Canadian unit that had not fought in the Second Battle of Ypres.

The PPCLI held Bellewaarde Ridge, northeast of the village of Hooge and south of Frezenberg. On May 8, the Germans attacked the British positions on the Frezenberg Ridge and captured Frezenberg village. The position of the PPCLI was a difficult one as its northern flank was exposed to German attack. Nevertheless, the men held out against repeated German attacks and were gradually reinforced by other units of the 27th Division. The 550 men who had begun the battle were relieved, finally, about midnight. They had suffered 397 casualties.

The Second Battle of Ypres continued until May 25. The final toll for all the British forces (including the Canadians) was 59,000 killed, wounded, taken prisoner and missing. Six thousand of those were Canadians, 2,000 of them dead.

ITINERARY: DURATION 4 HOURS

THE SECOND BATTLE OF YPRES – APRIL TO MAY, 1915

Point 1: The left of the Canadian line; gas is released April 22, 1915

Point 2: The attack on Kitcheners Wood, the night of April 22/23, 1915

Point 3: The attack of the 1st and 4th Battalions on Mauser Ridge April 23, 1915

Point 4: The Battle of St. Julien April 24, 1915

Point 5: The battle for Gravenstafel Ridge April 24/25, 1915

Point 6: The right of the Canadian line

Point 7: The Princess Patricia's Canadian Light Infantry at the Battle of Frezenberg Ridge May 8, 1915

THE SECOND BATTLE OF YPRES

The Tour

(You will notice some difference in spelling of place names. The names used during the First World War were French, whereas today the road signs are in Flemish. Please refer to the list at the beginning of this book. This text uses the French spellings from 1915.)

The tour begins in the Grote Markt in Ypres. Follow the one-way system of the Grote Markt, exiting towards the northeast left of the hotel de ville. Follow the signs to Poelcappelle and Roulers. You will pass through St. Jean and Wieltje.

Canadian troops were encamped in these villages as support for the front line in the event of an attack. As this area had been quiet for some time, the troops were not expecting any action. After the attack of April 22, chaos reigned in the towns which were packed with refugees, wounded, artillery and soldiers going up the line or retreating. After the battle, these villages were incorporated into the front line.

After you have passed through Wieltje, turn right at the junction and follow the road to Poelcappelle and Roulers.

After four kilometres, you will pass a small Commonwealth
War Graves cemetery on your left (Seaforth, Cheddar Villa).
Continue through the village of St. Julien towards the hamlet of
Keerselaere. You will arrive at Vancouver Crossroads and the
Canadian battle memorial, *The Brooding Soldier*, 6½ kilometres
from the Grote Markt. Continue on to Poelcappelle.

In the village centre is a stork statue, a work raised in memory
of the famous French air ace, Georges Guyemner, killed near
here in 1917.

Head out of the village back towards St. Julien, stopping 500
metres outside of Poelcappelle.

Point 1: The left of the Canadian line; gas is released April 22, 1915

This road marks the junction between the Canadian and
French lines. The Canadian line ran in a southeasterly direction
along the ridge visible to the south of the road. Fortifications
were not elaborate — a number of sand-bagged, half moon positions linked by the occasional shallow trench. The Canadians
were dismayed by the state of the defences when they came into
the line on April 18, but managed to make some improvements.

The units in the line were the 13th and 15th Battalions, whose
left flank was where you are now standing. The middle distance
was held by the 8th Battalion, commanded by Louis Lipsett, and
the right of the line by the 5th Battalion. Their right sat on the
Gravenstafel-Passchendaele road, four kilometres across the field
to the south. The Germans were 75 metres away.

Further south towards Ypres, but before the hamlet of
Keerselaere, elements of the 13th Battalion (under the command of Frederick Loomis) supported the brigade in the line.
West of St. Julien, the 14th Battalion was positioned in support of
the front line. The French Colonials held the defences north of
the salient (north of the road). Their position ran across the
fields east of Langemarck village.

At 5 p.m. on Thursday, April 22, the Canadians identified
the clouds moving westwards towards Langemarck as the
German secret weapon, poison gas, a weapon no one had faced

NORSWORTHY, EDWARD CUTHBERT, Major, 13th Battn. (Royal Highlanders of Canada), 3rd Brigade, Canadian Expeditionary Force, eldest *s.* of James Counter Norsworthy, of Ingersoll, P. Ontario, Canada, by his wife, Mary Jane, eldest dau. of Alexander Cuthbert, of Ingersoll, and gdson. of John Norsworthy, of the Parish of Widdicombe, co. Devon, England (who went to Canada in 1852); *b.* Ingersoll afsd., 29 May, 1879; killed in action in the Battle of Langemarck on 22 May, 1915; educ. Ingersoll and St. Thomas' Public Schools, from which he passed to the Upper Canada College, and thence matriculated to McGill University, at which time he won the Governor-General's gold medal for mathematics. He subsequently became registered as a Student of the Institute of Actuaries of Great Britain along with his younger brother Stanley. At the examination held that year, there were thirty-six candidates writing in the Dominion; of this number five were successful, including Major Norsworthy and his brother. In his student days he had been connected with the Cadet Corps at St. Thomas' Collegiate Institute, and the Upper Canada College Rifle Corps. Deciding to adopt a career in the financial world, he obtained a position with Messrs. G. A. Stimson & Co., of Toronto, and in 1901 he opend an office in Montreal as Manager for the Dominion Securities Corporation. He joined the 5th Royal Highlanders as a subaltern, shortly after his arrival there, and after passing his examination at St. John's (Quebec) Military School, he became Capt. in 1905, and Adjutant three years later, and Major in 1909. On the outbreak of war, Major Norsworthy volunteered his services, and helped to organise the 13th Battn. for active service, and accompanied it to Europe as Senior Major and Second in Command. While in England, he was offered an appointment with Sir Max Aitken, the Canadian "Eye Witness," but preferred to remain with his regt.; *unm.* On 22 April, 1915, the Germans, using virulent and asphyxiating gases for the first time, were able to overcome a portion of the French troops adjoining our line. In the words of Sir John French's Despatch of 15 June, 1915: "The left flank of the Canadian Division was thus left dangerously exposed to serious attack in flank, and there appeared to be a prospect of their being overwhelmed, and of a successful attempt by the Germans to cut off the British troops occupying the salient to the east. In spite of the danger to which they were exposed, the Royal Highlanders of Canada held their ground with a magnificent display of tenacity and courage ; and it is not too much to say that the bearing and conduct of these splendid troops averted a disaster which might have been attended with the most serious consequences." The 13th Battn. (5th Royal Highlanders) were the first Canadian troops to meet a charge of the Germans, and notwithstanding they were greatly outnumbered, and were being attacked in flank in their dug-outs, Major Norsworthy skilfully led his men out to the Ypres-Poelcapelle Road, manning the road ditches facing the advancing Germans, and heroically holding their position, and refusing to give one inch of ground, thereby setting the pace for the whole division. Major Norsworthy's part in the action was thus described by one of the privates present : "After having remained in the dug-outs for about one hour, with our throats parched and our eyes watering, caused by the gas, we could see that the Germans had broken our lines. It was reported to Major Norsworthy, and he gave the order to 'stand to' which we were waiting anxiously to do, and he led us out to the Ypres-Poelcapelle Road. It was not long before they began to pick our boys off. Major Norsworthy was hit in the neck by a bullet, but it did not stop him from walking up and down our line, encouraging our men to hold fast. It was not until he received the second bullet that he had to give in and lie down. We bound him up as well as we could, but the second wound was serious, and he died about three-quarters of an hour after." Another private who was with Major Norsworthy said : "As we advanced out of our dug-outs and trenches—that were being enfiladed—we met a perfect storm of shell and rifle bullets, when some inclinations of hesitancy and flinching were shown. Seeing this, Major Nors-

Edward C. Norsworthy.

worthy sprang to the front and called out, 'Come on, men, remember that we are Canadians and all the eyes of Canada are upon us.' His action and words steadied those that were wavering, and we all followed him with a wild cheer, and advanced to the Ypres-Poelcapelle Road ditches—facing the advancing Germans—which gave us some little protection, and we stuck it there to the last man." The following are extracts spoken to the first Canadian Division after the twelve days and nights of fighting included in the period from 22 of April to the 4th of May, 1915 : "I tell you truly that my heart is so full I hardly know how to speak to you. It is full of sorrow for the loss of those comrades of ours who have gone, and pride in what the first Canadian Division has done. I think it is possible that you do not all of you quite realise that if we had retired in the evening of 22 April, when our Allies fell back before the gas and left our left flank quite open, the whole of the 27th and 28th Division would probably have been cut off. This is what our Commander-in-Chief meant when he telegraphed as he did : 'The Canadians saved the situation.' My lads, if ever men have had a right to be praised in this work, you have." Major Norsworthy was mentioned in F.M. Sir John (now Lord) French's Despatch of 31 May, 1915, for gallant and distinguished service in the field.

before. In the face of the suffocating gas the defenceless French troops, not surprisingly, panicked and rapidly abandoned their forward positions. They streamed towards Ypres leaving a gap on the left of the Canadian line, which extended from the Ypres-Poelcappelle road where you stand, to the Ypres Canal six kilometres west.

From this point, it is not hard to imagine that poisonous cloud rolling across the fields blinding, suffocating and choking the vulnerable French troops in their disorderly retreat.

The Canadians in the field responded quickly. The 13th Battalion extended its line across the road to investigate the French positions. Discovering the empty defensive positions and the terrorized troops, Major Norsworthy commanded his men to set up defensive positions north of the Poelcappelle Road.

As the gas cleared, the Germans slowly advanced towards the vacated French positions, some troops veering to the right to deal with fire from the 13th and 15th Battalions. They continued to attack the advance positions and finally overwhelmed them, killing Norsworthy and Lieutenant Guy Drummond. The Canadians' flanking fire, however, was sufficient to drive the Germans westward in pursuit of easier targets.

Canada's first Victoria Cross of the Great War was awarded for an action performed during this battle. Fred Fisher of Montreal, a soldier in the 13th Battalion, was part of the defensive flank set up during the German attack. Advancing from St. Julien, Lance Corporal Fisher observed the Germans advancing steadily towards the guns of a Canadian field artillery battery.

Directly west of where you are standing, he set up his machine gun in front of the guns and held off the Germans until the gunners could escape. Four of the six men in his crew were killed. Afterwards, Fisher advanced to the front line and continued fighting. He was killed on the open flank the next day and his body was never recovered.

Canadian Brigade commanders, aware of the size of the gap and its threat to the troops, knew the break had to be sealed. Canadian support troops moved into the fields north of St. Julien and harassed the German advance in a ferocious shelling action.

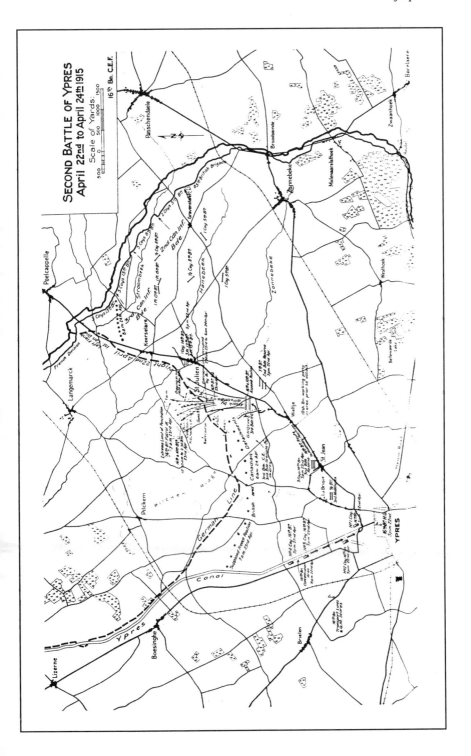

The Battle of Ypres

The 14th Battalion of Montreal at St. Julien and St. Jean advanced north of the village to fill the northern part of the gap left by the French. The 7th Battalion reinforced the positions south of and in the village of St. Julien. But the gaping left flank remained open and further action had to be taken to prevent a catastrophe.

The units along the Ypres-Poelcappelle road were able to hold fast on April 22 and 23 but the following day, the Germans attacked with gas again and in such force that the Canadian positions became graves! The 13th and 15th Battalions retreated to St. Julien.

Return to your car and drive back through St. Julien, passing the Canadian monument en route. Keep an eye for Seaforth Cemetery (Cheddar Villa) on the right side of the road one kilometre south of the village. Enter the cemetery and go to its north end.

Point 2: The attack on Kitcheners Wood, the night of April 22/23, 1915

Kitchener's Wood (which no longer exists) was a large copse one kilometre northwest of this point. The Germans had captured it from the French on April 22, gaining an excellent position to launch an attack to cut off Canadian and British forces positioned deep in the salient to the south. In addition, the flank from St. Julien to Ypres was still open.

The Third Canadian Brigade received orders to attack the wood on the evening of April 22. But by the time the 10th and 16th Battalions moved up from St. Jean and were in position, it was nearly midnight. The situation was desperate and confusing as inexperienced Canadian soldiers prepared to attack a position they had never seen before, and at night. They formed up for the attack in the field to your left.

At midnight, they proceeded as quietly as possible across the open fields to attack a German position in the wood. They continued to advance undetected until they stumbled into a hedge in the middle distance. The noise of the hundreds of troops pushing their way through the hedge betrayed them.

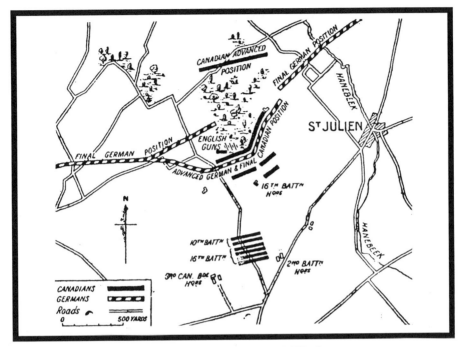

The Attack on Kitchener's Wood

The Germans opened fire. The Canadians charged, fell and cried out. Pure courage pushed them onward into the wood and enabled them to clear most of it through severe hand-to-hand fighting and advance into the fields to the north. The losses for both the Albertans and the Scottish were heavy and included the commander of the 10th Battalion, Lieutenant Colonel Russell Boyle of Crossfield, Alberta, who was mortally wounded. The dead men, kilted or in khaki, lay strewn across the field.

The Germans managed to retain a few positions within the wood and the Canadians, realizing they could not hold the wood itself or the outposts north of it, finally retreated to hastily dug trenches south of the wood, about 200 metres north of where you stand. This exposed position was vulnerable and subjected to systematic pounding by the Germans throughout April 23 and 24. Both battalions, shattered by the attack, were relieved piece-meal on April 23 by the 3rd and 2nd Battalions. The survivors were withdrawn.

The success of the attack on Kitchener's Wood had surprised the Germans and secured a further position of the open left flank, which was still open from the wood to the Ypres Canal. The relieving soldiers from the 2nd and 3rd Battalions reinforced the other Canadians at St. Julien, but still their position was precarious.

Surprisingly, the Germans failed to exploit the success of their secret weapon on April 23. The British and Canadians, on the other hand, could not afford to wait. The flank had to be secured. The other Canadian reserve units had yet to be committed. April 23 was to be their day.

Return to your car and turn back towards Ypres. After 500 metres, you will see signs for three Commonwealth War Graves cemeteries: Buffs Road, Track X and No Mans Cot. Turn right on to the side road and drive past the cemeteries. You will come to three more Commonwealth War Graves cemeteries after about two kilometres: New Irish Farm, Divisional Collecting Post Extension and La Belle Alliance. Continue straight for 600 metres where the road ends at the Pilckem road. Turn right and drive on for one kilometre. Stop your car.

Point 3: The attack of the 1st and 4th Battalions on Mauser Ridge April 23, 1915

The ridge you followed past the cemeteries was known as Hilltop Ridge in 1915. It was held by the British and Canadians throughout the battle. The ridge in front of you as you drove along Pilckem Road was known as Mauser Ridge. This ridge was taken on April 22 by the Germans, who proceeded to dig in, set up barbed wire and prepare their defences. Although you are now standing in an industrial estate, the area of the battlefields off to the east between Hilltop and Mauser ridges is still open farmland.

Many of the farms you see were objectives of the Canadian attack of April 23 and of frontal, daylight attacks by the British and Indians in the following days. They remain in the same locations as they were in 1915, although the original farm buildings were likely reduced to splinters by the end of 1915.

The First Canadian Infantry Brigade had been held in reserve west of Ypres. The 1st, 2nd, 3rd and 4th Battalions were the reserve troops of the Canadian Division. Already the 2nd and 3rd Battalions were reinforcing the open flank at Kitchener's Wood and St. Julien. Now the 1st and 4th Battalions were asked to capture the German positions on Mauser Ridge. In broad daylight!

It is hard to say which Canadian attack, Mauser Ridge or Kitchener's Wood, was most ill-conceived. The Canadians were to attack east of the Pilckem Road, jumping off from where you turned off onto the Pilckem road. The two battalions, roughly 2,000 men strong, attacked at 5:25 a.m. The advance went smoothly as the leading waves crossed the shallow valley, but then all hell broke loose and the Canadians were stopped in their tracks. British troops attacking on the Canadian right captured Turco Farm (the large farm 500 metres due east of this point), but later retreated. The Canadians were pinned down in the shallow valley which stands before you.

At 4:25 p.m. they tried it again. Assisting a major attack by British and French units the 1st and 4th Battalions once again assaulted Mauser Ridge. Sadly they had the same lack of success they had had in the morning attack.

More than 850 Canadians were killed or wounded on the slopes of the Mauser Ridge, including the commanding officer of the 4th Battalion, Lieutenant Colonel Arthur Birchall. He was killed leading his men west of Turco Farm. His body was never recovered. For these losses the flank, opened by the gas on April 22, was closed. The Germans were not finished yet.

The British continued to attack the German positions in front of Pilckem. On April 26 the Lahore Division attacked across the shallow valley between Hilltop and Mauser ridges and, for small gains, were virtually annihilated.

Return down the Pilckem road, turn left and retrace the earlier route. Follow the road along Hilltop Ridge, past New Irish Farm Cemetery (where many of the men killed in the attack are buried), and past Buff Road Cemetery. Four hundred metres past the cemetery and just before rejoining the main road, a large farm appears on the left.

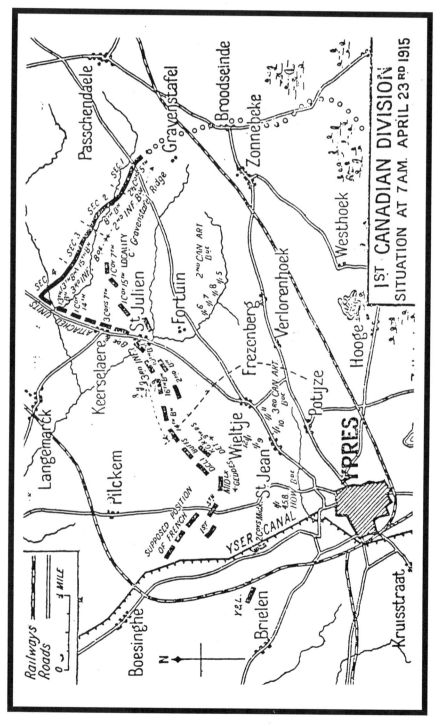

The Situation after the Counterattack April 23, 1915

This is Mouse Trap Farm, the headquarters of the 3rd Canadian Brigade and the scene of a heroic action by Captain Francis Scrimger of the Canadian Army Medical Corps. Scrimger was the Medical Officer of the 14th Battalion, tending to wounded at the farm. On April 25, heavy shelling of the farm had ignited the buildings which in turn ignited a small arms ammunition store also located in the farm, setting off the explosives. Scrimger directed the removal of the wounded throughout the explosions and then carried out a wounded Canadian officer. Under heavy fire he swam across the moat of the farm with the officer on his back. For his bravery, Captain Scrimger was awarded the Victoria Cross, the fourth awarded to Canadians in this battle.

Continue to the main road and turn left, driving towards St. Julien. Pass through the village and proceed to the Canadian memorial directly north of it. Leave your car in the car park and enter the battlefield park.

Point 4: The Battle of St. Julien April 24, 1915

Visibility from the Canadian monument is negligible. You will have a better view from the northwest corner of the park, reached by walking down the path through the shrubs. From here, you will see the crossroads leading to Langemarck (to the northwest) and Poelcappelle (to the north) and the locations of the actions of the battle of St. Julien on April 24.

Since the assault on the French, the Canadian line had not changed significantly. The 13th Battalion still held the apex, that is, the position running from the Ypres-Poelcappelle road, then cutting back sharply in a south-southwesterly direction to the fields north of St. Julien. Across the field, four kilometres from the Ypres-Poelcappelle road to the Gravenstafel-Passchendaele road, the 15th, the 8th and the 5th Battalions were in place awaiting the German attack. The Canadians were in the fields around St. Julien, south of where you stand, waiting for the next onslaught.

You should be able to see the church steeples of Langemarck (to the northwest) and of Poelcappelle (to the north). The Gravenstafel Ridge gently rises to the east.

HART-McHARG, WILLIAM FREDERICK RICHARD, Lieut.-Col., 7th Battn. (1st British Columbia Regt.) Canadian Expeditionary Force, only *s.* of the late Hon. Major William Hart-McHarg, 44th (Essex) Regt., by his wife, Jane Scott (10, Netherhall Gardens, N.W.), dau. of the late Capt. Thomsett, 44th Regt. ; *b.* Kilkenny, 16 Feb. 1869 ; educ. Bruges ; went to Canada about 1885 and was a Barrister-at-Law and Solicitor of the Supreme Court of British Columbia, practising at Vancouver, where he was a partner in the firm of Abbott, Hart-McHarg & Duncan. He joined the Canadian Militia about 1895 as a Private and rose to the command of the 7th (Vancouver) Regt., receiving the medal for 20 years' service. He served in the South African War, 1900-2, with the first contingent (Royal Canadian Regt.) and obtained the Queen's medal with four clasps (Paardeberg, Driefontein, Johannesburg and Cape Colony), and in 1911 was one of the Canadian contingent present at the Coronation of King George V. On the outbreak of the European War, Lieut.-Col. Hart-McHarg was given command of the 7th Regt. and came over with the first contingent and went to France in Feb. 1915. At the Second

W. F. R. Hart-McHarg.

Battle of Ypres, the 7th formed part of the 3rd Brigade, and on Friday, 23 April, occupied a position on the forward crest of a ridge, with its left flank near St. Julien. This position was severely shelled by the Germans during that day, and about 4.30 Col. Hart-McHarg, Major (now Lieut.-Col. Commanding) Odlum and Lieut. Mathewson, of the Canadian Engineers, went out to reconnoitre the ground. The exact location of the German forces opposed to them was not known, and they moved down the slope to the ruined village of Keerselaere—a distance of about 300 yards—in broad daylight without drawing a shot, but when they reached there they saw the Germans not 100 yards away, and they accordingly turned and began to retire. They were followed by a burst of rapid fire the moment they cleared the shelter of the ruins. Col. Hart-McHarg and Major Odlum managed to get into a shell-hole near by, but not before the former had been severely wounded. When Major Odlum discovered this, he raced up the hill under heavy fire in search of surgical aid. He found Capt. G. Gibson, Medical Officer, 7th Battn., who, accompanied by Sergt. J. Dryden, went down to the shell-hole immediately. They managed to move the Colonel into a ditch and there dressed his wound and remained with him till after dark, when he was carried back to Battn. Headquarters. He died the following day, 24 April, 1915, in hospital at Poperinghe, and was buried there in the New Cemetery with Col. Boyle, who fell the same day. He was mentioned in Despatches [London Gazette, 22 June, 1915] for gallant and distinguished conduct in the field. Col. Hart-McHarg was well known as a fine rifle shot. In 1908 he gained the Gold Medal of Canada after a close contest with three redoubtable antagonists from Toronto and Ottawa. He had shot several times in Canada's national teams, and had distinguished himself in the matches for the Palma International Trophy against the selected teams of the United States, Great Britain, Australia and other countries. He held the record individual score in the match, being in this respect a world's champion. He had also shot for Canada in the Empire Trophy match, founded by the Australians as an inter-Empire competition. He was a member of the Canadian team at Bisley in 1907, 1910 and 1914, and was spoken of as the next commandant of the Canadian team for Bisley. He shot for the Dominion here in both the Mackinnon and Kolapore Imperial matches, and in 1910 he tied for the Prince of Wales's Prize with the British Army champion, the famous Capt. Wallingford, who is now with the New Zealand Force. Each scored 85, the highest possible, with 17 bull's-eyes at 300 and 600 yards. Col Hart-McHarg lost on shooting off the tie, but he won the Bronze Cross ot the Bisley Grand Aggregate. In Aug. 1913, he won the Governor-General's prize for the second time—the Blue Riband—at the Dominion of Canada rifle meeting at Ottawa and the Long Range Championship of the World with army rifle at the international matches, Camp Perry, Ohio. He was *unm.*

Although difficult to understand the importance of the height (see *Point 5),* this ridge was the backbone of the Canadian defence. The men of the 7th Battalion were dug in along the ridge and reinforced with spare Canadian troops. Particularly well defended was the high point on the ridge, Locality "C".

April 23 had been a quiet day in the terms of attacks, although German shelling of the open positions was heavy. Disturbed by the shelling, 7th Battalion commander Lieutenant Colonel William Hart-McHarg decided to reconnoitre the ground 300 metres ahead of the 7th's position on the ridge. Accompanied by two of his officers, he approached the apparently abandoned buildings of Keerselaere. From one of the buildings, he observed parties of Germans less than 100 metres away and tried to make a quick escape. Hart-McHarg was mortally wounded. He was 46.

At 4 a.m. on April 24 the Germans, using chlorine gas, attacked the Canadian positions from the Ypres-Poelcappelle road along the Canadian front. The 8th Battalion held firm, but the concentration was too much for the 15th.

Overwhelmed, the men were either killed or captured, leaving a huge gap in the centre of the Canadian position. If you look towards Poelcappelle, you will see where the Canadians retreated across the fields towards St. Julien, the poisonous gas burning their throats and stinging their eyes, even this far behind the front.

The Germans took full advantage of this, attacking the Canadian positions in front of St. Julien from the rear and towards the western toe of the Gravenstafel Ridge. St. Julien was surrounded and many men taken prisoner. The fighting for St. Julien continued for most of the day. British attempts to take the village in daylight succeeded in only stemming the German advance.

Walk along the outer perimeter of the park as far as the eastern corner. From here you can see the western toe of the Gravenstafel Ridge.

THE SAINT JULIEN MEMORIAL

In 1920, after some consideration of whether, and how, Canada should commemorate its contribution to The Great War, it was decided to honor the exploits of the Canadian Forces.

Eight sites were chosen:

St. Julien
Passchendaele (Crest Farm)
Hill 62 (Mont Sorrel)
Hill 145 (Vimy)
Dury Crossroads (Drocourt-Queant line)
Bourlon Wood (Canal-du-Nord, Cambrai)
Courcelette (Somme)
Hospital Wood (Amiens)

After obtaining the sites, through donation or purchase, Canada then considered how best to commemorate — would it be eight equal memorials or one main memorial and seven smaller ones? Finally, a competition was held for Canadian architects, the results of which so impressed the committee that the government's plans were changed.

Walter Allward's design for Vimy and Frederick Clemesha's for St. Julien were accepted and a decision made to place 13-tonne blocks of granite on the other six sites.

"The Brooding Soldier" (11 metres high and made of granite) was unveiled north of St. Julien on July 8, 1923, by H. R. H. The Duke of Connaught. The crowd was addressed by Lieutenant General Sir Richard Turner, VC, commander of the 3rd Brigade at Ypres and, following the ceremony, lunch was served at Skindles Hotel in Ypres. The memorial park remains impressive today in spite of the shrubs and trees which obstruct the views. Perhaps in time, these will be removed.

I still wonder why the memorial was not located at Locality "C" on Gravenstafel Ridge.

THIS·COLUMN·MARKS·THE
BATTLEFIELD·WHERE·18.000
CANADIANS·ON·THE·BRITISH
LEFT·WITHSTOOD·THE·FIRST
GERMAN·GAS·ATTACKS·THE
22–24·APRIL·1915·2.000·FELL
AND·LIE·BURIED·NEARBY

(PHOTO N. CHRISTIE)

Plaque on St. Julien Memorial

After the successful cracking of the 15th Battalion, the Germans attacked the ridge. The defenders on the toe slowed the advance, while the machine guns of the 7th Battalion took a heavy toll of the attacking Germans. Their bravery saved the Canadians.

The machine gun crews performed exceptionally well and Lieutenant Edward Bellew was awarded the Victoria Cross for his bravery on the ridge. Wounded, Bellew was one of the 267 men of the 7th Battalion taken prisoner during the battle.

Another 176 men of the 7th Battalion died. More than 60 of their bodies were found in small cemeteries at the foot of the ridge when the battlefields were cleared after the war.

As the Germans pressed along the ridge, the 7th Battalion and its assortment of reinforcements were finally overwhelmed.

Return to your car, turn left on the road to Gravenstafel (New Zealand memorial), then turn left again onto the *first* small road. This will take you past a windmill, the old version of which was the command post of the 15th Canadians during the battle. You are on the Gravenstafel Ridge and if you look to the north you will be looking over the Canadian front-line trenches, where Canadians of the 8th and 15th Battalions hung on for their lives on April 24 and 25, 1915. Their front line was on the first ridge you see to the north across the fields. The importance of this height will become obvious as you ascend the Gravenstafel Ridge. Ypres is south. This area fell to the Germans on April 24. Continue along the ridge for 2¼ kilometres and stop at the high point. The view from here is excellent.

Point 5: The battle for Gravenstafel Ridge April 24/25, 1915

This was Locality "C", the backbone of the Canadian defences. From here you can see, to the east, Passchendaele Church, Tyne Cot British Cemetery and the chimneys of the Zonnebeke brickyard. To the north is the church of Poelcappelle, to the west the windmill and Langemarck Church, and to the south you will see Ypres and the Monts des Flandres.

Towards Poelcappelle is the area of the Canadian front line, from the Ypres-Poelcappelle road to the Gravenstafel-Passchendaele road where the Canadian battalions held against the Germans.

Edward Munden Dwyer.

DWYER, EDWARD MUNDEN, Private, No. 1077, 8th Battn. Canadian Expeditionary Force, *s.* of John Thomas Dwyer, of Ignace, Ontario, Canada (originally from co. Tipperary); *b.* Ignace, 24 Nov. 1887; educ. there; was for some years in the Mechanical Dept. of the C.P.R., and was then transferred to the Traffic Dept., and when war broke out was a Conductor. He enlisted 20 Aug. 1914, came over with the first contingent in Oct., and after training on Salisbury Plain during the winter, went to France, and was killed in action at Festubert, 23 April, 1915; *unm.*

GOMES, MANOEL ANTONIO, Gunner, No. 40530, 2nd Battery, 1st Field Artillery Brigade, Canadian Expeditionary Force, eldest *s.* of Manoel Gomes Beinhos, of the Island of Madeira, by his wife, Joqina, dau. of Antonio de Jesus, of Nossa Senhora da Monte, Madeira, and nephew of Manuel de Jesus, of 14, Pitt Street, New Amsterdam, Berbice, British Guiana, Merchant; *b.* Madeira, 24 May, 1892; went to British Guiana in 1902 and entered the employ of his uncle there; joined the B.G. Militia (No. 2291, No. 7 Coy.), 5 Oct. 1909; went to Canada, 5 May, 1913, and entered the Ontario Business College in Belleville, and on leaving there obtained a post with the Grand Trunk Railway; volunteered on the outbreak of the European War in Aug. 1914 and joined the Canadian Expeditionary Force; left for England with the 34th Battery in the first contingent Oct. 1914; went to France in Feb. and was killed in action at the second Battle of Ypres, 24 April, 1915, a shell bursting directly under his horse, when bringing up ammunition.

Manoel Antonio Gomes.

He was buried near the wagon lines between the Brielen Road and the Yser Canal, and a cross with his name, etc., was erected by his comrades. He was *unm*

CHIVAS, EDWIN JOHN, Private, No. 27051, 15th Battn. (48th Canadian Highlanders), Canadian Expeditionary Force, *s.* of William Hay Chivas, of 74, Chisley Avenue, London, Ontario (who served for 16 years in the 3rd Battn. Gordon Highlanders and then settled in Canada), *b.* Fraserburgh, co. Aberdeen; educ. there; went to Canada with his parents in 1901; volunteered on the outbreak of war in Aug. 1914; left with the first Contingent in Oct.; went to the Front in Feb., and was killed in action at St. Julien, Belgium, 24 April, 1915; *unm.* Sergt. L. D. Anderson, A. Coy. 15th Battn., who was invalided back to Canada after this action, gave the following account: " I was in charge of the fort in which he was, and we retired together after being forced out by the gas fumes in the Battle of St. Julien, 24 April. Twenty or more of us lay all day under a terrible shell fire, being unconscious for most of the time, from early morning—5 o'clock—till dusk. At dusk, I being the senior, and having come to my senses, decided that we must start to gain shelter or else we should all be lost, as our breathing was coming harder and I felt I was becoming worse.

Edwin John Chivas.

I crawled over to him and braced him up, with my arms around him, telling him that we would try to get across two fields to a road ; here I felt we might get water or aid. Your son's strength had so far gone that he could walk but a very few paces and then dropped to the ground. Whether he died then or later I cannot tell you, as I, with two others, forced my way till I lay exhausted, only to be rescued by two artillerymen and brought back to life in the hospital. Your son was very much beloved by all his comrades and always was cheery and happy. We slept side by side for a long time, and so I knew him very well. When on several occasions, as I was accustomed to read from the ' Book ' on Sundays, I forgot, your son would remind me, and our little group would sit in a quiet corner and have a quiet read of some of St. Paul or the Ninety-first Psalm. Your son was a good and true soldier." His three brothers are all on active service, two with the Divisional Ammunition Column, and the third as a baker in the A.S.C.

It was on April 24, when the German gas and artillery broke the 15th Battalion (towards the Ypres-Poelcappelle road), that this area became chaotic. Imagine the gas clouds rolling across the fields and the terror of the vulnerable troops. In the centre the 8th Battalion held firm against the gas and artillery, stopping the German infantry cold. They even tried to cover the flank left open by the retreating 15th Battalion. The 5th Battalion never had to face the gas directly but performed tremendously throughout the battle.

Late on April 24, the Germans, fighting down the length of the ridge, captured Locality "C", but were unable to capture the next farm on the ridge, at the bend — Boetleer's Farm (the headquarters of Lieutenant Colonel Louis Lipsett, the exceptional commander of the 8th Battalion). At the end of the day's fighting the 8th and 5th Battalions were still in their original positions but the situation had become impossible. On the following day, both battalions, under heavy pressure from the Germans, withdrew to the ridge and to the hamlet of Gravenstafel itself.

The bravery of the men of the 8th Battalion cannot be overstated. Their performance, and that of Colonel Lipsett, was the outstanding achievement of the Canadians in the Second Battle of Ypres. Another example of this bravery was Company Sergeant Major Frederick Hall's attempt during the confusion of April 24 to bring in a wounded comrade who was lying in the open. Ignoring the heavy German fire and the obvious risk to himself, Hall approached the wounded man and was killed. For his bravery, he was awarded the Victoria Cross.[2] His body was never recovered.

The remnants of the Canadian battalions remained on the ridge until relieved on April 26. It surprises me the Canadian Government did not put the Canadian Battlefield Memorial at this location after the war.

---

[2] Two other men besides Hall, all from the same street in Winnipeg, won Victoria Crosses with the Canadian Expeditionary Force. Leo Clarke VC and R. Shankland VC are the others. The street where they lived is now called Valour Road.

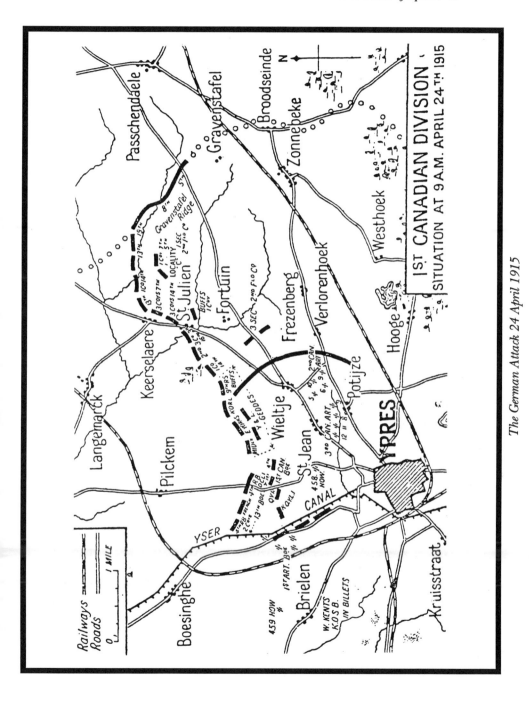

The German Attack 24 April 1915

1ST CANADIAN DIVISION
SITUATION AT 9 A.M. APRIL 24TH 1915

Return to your car and proceed to the Gravenstafel cross-roads. Turn left beside the New Zealand memorial (Battle of Broodseinde, October 4, 1917). Continue up the Passchendaele road and stop about 50 metres past the calvary on your left.

Point 6: The right of the Canadian line

The right flank of the 5th Canadians was secured immediately north of this road. Their position ran northwest towards Poelcappelle — the church steeple to the north marks the village — near to where the gas was released against the 15th Battalion on April 24. It was here the 15th was forced to retreat down the Ypres-Poelcappelle road, surrendering the apex and exposing the flank of the 8th Battalion immediately to the left of the 5th Battalion.

The 8th's position ran across the ridge to your right, halfway to Poelcappelle. The 8th and 5th Battalions had remained in their original positions since April 22.

They came under direct frontal attack on April 25 and their position was also threatened by the German's attack along the Gravenstafel Ridge and capture of Locality "C". They were eventually forced to withdraw on April 25 and made a fighting retreat to the Canadian-held positions on the eastern end of the Gravenstafel Ridge near the New Zealand monument.

Sadly, the lessons of this war were not understood in 1915. The same Canadian Expeditionary Force was here again in October 1917. Jump-off lines for the disastrous battle of Passchendaele were only 250 metres further along the Gravenstafel-Passchendaele road.

For the Canadians, the April 25 retreat to the ridge marked the end of the more severe fighting. On April 26 they were withdrawn from the line to reserve positions. Although they were involved in some frontline activity until early May, it was primarily as carrying parties. There were some casualties, but for the most part the Second Battle of Ypres was over.

British troops continued to fight, making several counter-attacks near St. Julien and towards Pilckem, but they achieved little. The ground conceded was not recovered until the Third Battle of Ypres, July–August 1917.

Return to your car and retrace your path to Ypres.

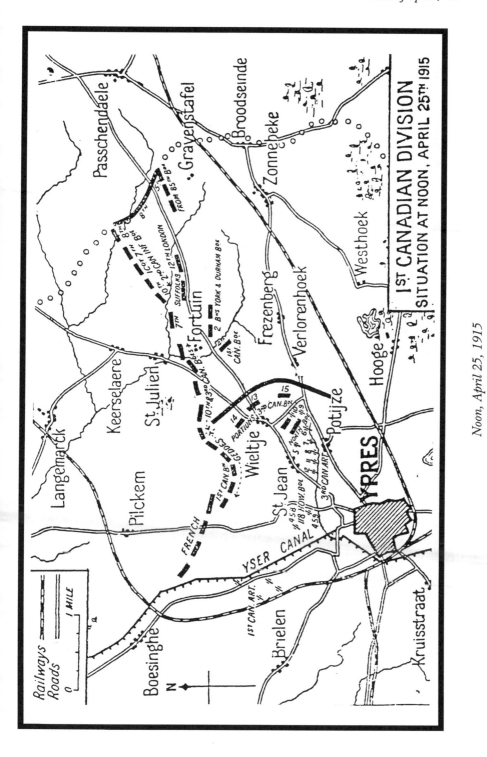

Noon, April 25, 1915

Point 7: The Princess Patricia's Canadian Light Infantry at the Battle of Frezenberg Ridge May 8, 1915

The first Canadian unit to enter the line was the PPCLI. Privately raised and composed primarily of former regular soldiers, the PPCLI was part of the 80th Infantry Brigade of the 27th Imperial Division. They entered the front lines in December 1914 and, during the start of the Second Battle of Ypres, held a position east of Zonnebeke in the southern half of the Ypres Salient. They withdrew from the trenches near Zonnebeke on May 4, 1915 and were in position just west of Westhoek on the Frezenberg Ridge by May 8.

Starting from the Grote Markt at Ypres, follow the main road towards Menin. Continue past Hooge and turn left 50 metres beyond the Bellewaarde Amusement Park, following signs to the PPCLI memorial. Go through Westhoek and turn left when you see signposts for the memorial.

Erected in 1958, this memorial marks the PPCLI's heroic stand, when they "counted not the cost", on Bellewaarde Ridge May 8, 1915. The ridge is directly east of the wood and north of the amusement park (you will see the park's taller rides).

The PPCLI withdrew to this position as part of a general withdrawal on May 4. It had scarcely arrived before heavy German fire inflicted more than a hundred casualties.

On the morning of May 8, the Germans frontally assaulted the 28th Imperial Division north of the PPCLI. Within three hours they had broken through the British line and begun to roll up the British on either flank. The PPCLI refused to budge and drove back each German attack with heavy losses but it was eventually forced to withdraw from the main trench on the crest of the ridge. Essentially cut off, the PPCLI held out for 17 hours, preventing the Germans from rolling up the centre of the British line.

In spite of heavy losses, the PPCLI refused to leave their wounded and clung on to the exposed position. Sister units in the brigade came to their assistance supplying ammunition and some reinforcements. Late on May 8, the survivors were

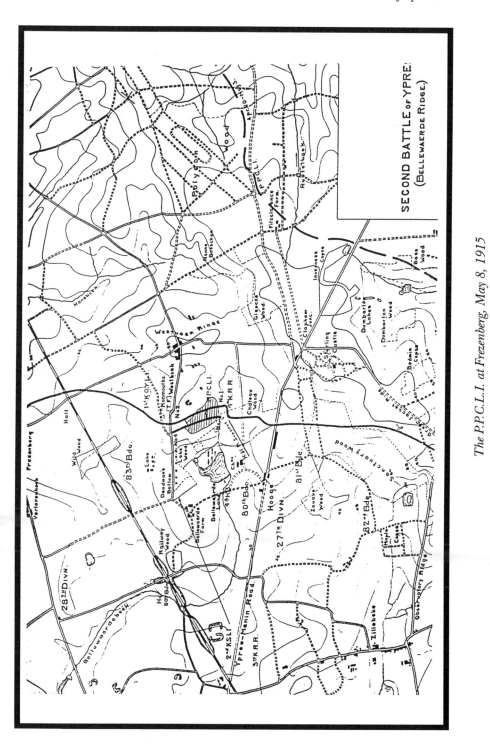

The P.P.C.L.I. at Frezenberg, May 8, 1915

withdrawn to Ypres. Of the 550 men who had entered the battle, 397 were casualties.

The position was relinquished in a general retirement and not recaptured until the Third Battle of Passchendaele in July 1917.

To return to Ypres, go back to the Menin road and turn right.

WALLER, HORACE EDMUND, Private, No. 1530, Princess Patricia's Canadian Light Infantry, yr. *s.* of John Edward Hopkins Waller, of Rockvale, co. Tipperary, 172, Cromwell Road, London, S.W., and The Nook, Westgate-on-Sea, M.Inst.C.E., by his wife, Annette Elizabeth, dau. of Adolphe Naudé, and grandson of the late John Francis Waller, of Finoe House, co. Tipperary, LL.D., J.P., Barrister-at-Law, writer and poet ; *b.* in London, 16 April, 1891 ; educ. the Towers, Wellington College, and Tonbridge School (Scholar), and on leaving there entered the Engineering Section of the University of London at King's College, and was one of the earliest members of the O.T.C. In 1910 he went to Canada where he engaged in engineering, the principal work with which he was connected being the Hydro Electric installation of the Algoma Central Railway at Steep Hill Falls, Ontario, and the government survey of Strathcona Park, Vancouver Island, B.C. On the declaration of war he joined the 1st Contingent of Princess Patricia's Canadian L.I. as a private, and after training in Canada, on Salisbury Plain, and at Winchester, left Southampton for France with his regt. to join the Expeditionary Force on Sunday, 20 Dec. 1914. Owing to his intimate knowledge of French and his experience as an engineer, he was detailed to act as interpreter and guide. He was frequently in the trenches, and although as a result of the severe conditions prevailing he developed dysentery, he would not be persuaded to rest. On 4 Feb., however, he was obliged to enter hospital at Boeschèpe, and he died there, 7 Feb. 1915 ; *unm.* He was buried in the churchyard at Boeschèpe with full military honours. Lieut. Crabbe wrote : " I must tell you as one of his company officers how great a loss to No. 4 he is. He was always an excellent soldier, and seemed to thoroughly realise how his superior education and position necessitated his being a good example, and in this he never failed. Since we have been actually fighting he was of great service as a company guide, and invariably showed the greatest courage and devotion to duty"; and Sergt. Phillips : " Everybody in No. 4 Coy. and anybody in other companies who knew him join you in mourning the loss of one of the best little fellows that ever lived, and one whom I am very proud to have called friend. He was the most popular man in the company."

Horace Edmund Waller.

EARDLEY - WILMOT, FREDERICK LAWRENCE, Lieut., Princess Patricia's Canadian L.I., only *s.* of Col. Arthur Eardley-Wilmot, of Westernlea, Westward Ho ! and Hales Hall, Cheadle, co Staffordshire, late R.F.A., by his wife, Mary Blanche, only dau. of Clement Thomas Sneyd-Kynnersley, of Loxley Park, and Highfields, co. Stafford, and grandson of Major-Gen. Frederick Marrow Eardley-Wilmot, R.A. [2nd son of Sir John Eardley-Wilmot, 1st Bart.]; *b.* Portsmouth, 25 Feb. 1895 ; educ. Cheltenham and Toronto University (Oct. 1913 to Aug. 1914) ; volunteered on the outbreak of war and was gazetted Lieut., P.P.C.L.I. 22 Sept. 1914 ; came over with the first contingent in Oct. 1914 ; was appointed Machine Gun Officer, Feb. ; went to France when his regt. joined the 20th Brigade (27th Division), and was killed in action in the trenches at St. Eloi, 18 March, 1915 ; *unm.*

SWEETMAN, JOHN STANLEY, Capt., Toronto Home Guards, Canadian Militia, 3rd *s.* of Edward Sweetman, late of Ryde, I.W., Brewer, by his wife, Emily (42, Priory Road, Hampstead, N.W.), dau. of the late William Godden, of East Street, Southampton ; *b.* Ryde, 28 July, 1890 ; educ. Ryde Upper Grade School ; was an Accountant in the Bloor Bathurst Street Branch of the Home Bank of Canada ; joined the Toronto Home Guards after the outbreak of war in Aug. 1914, and died in the General Hospital, Toronto, 12 Oct. 1914, from cerebral-spinal meningitis, contracted while undergoing a course of training ; *unm.*

John Stanley Sweetman.

JAMES WILLIAM DAMES, DCM
Princess Patricia's Canadian Light Infantry

When war was declared in August 1914, Canada had a permanent military force of only 3,000 men. The enthusiasm for this new war, however, sent Canadians, many recent immigrants to the country, flocking to join the colors.

People from all walks of life were infected with this enthusiasm, including Canada's magnates of commerce, who had money and political connections. One of these men, Montreal millionaire Hamilton Gault, offered to raise a battalion at his own expense, and in August 1914 the Princess Patricia's Canadian Light Infantry was formed in Landsdowne Park in Ottawa.

The PPCLI was different from others being formed then. It was rife with ex-British regular soldiers who had fought in The Sudan, South Africa or one of the many colonial actions that had taken place at the end of Queen Victoria's reign. In nine days, 1,098 men were recruited to the unit, 1,049 of them with previous service and 771 of them wearing campaign medals. Ninety per cent of the recruits were from the British Isles.

Typical of these men was Company Sergeant Major James Dames, DCM. Born in London, England in 1871, Dames enlisted at the age of 14 and served in India and South Africa. In the Boer War, he was wounded twice and awarded the Distinguished Conduct Medal. In 1909, he emigrated to Canada and settled in Alberta.

With the PPCLI, he went to France in December 1914. He was killed at Bellewaarde Ridge on May 8, 1915 at the age of 44, but his body was not recovered. In 1925, a battlefield clearance discovered the remains of two unknown Canadian soldiers on Bellewaarde Ridge. One soldier's uniform, however, held the medal ribbons of the Distinguished Conduct Medal, the Queen's and King's South Africa medals. The body was buried in Hagle Dump Cemetery near Ypres and a headstone to an unknown Canadian was raised over the grave.

A reevaluation of the original documents confirmed this as Dames's grave in 1992. In 1994, a headstone bearing his name and regimental details was erected over his grave. The chapter was closed after 77 years!

James W. Dames.

DAMES, JAMES WILLIAM, D.C.M., Sergt.-Major, No. 1315, Princess Patricia's Canadian Light Infantry, 2nd *s.* of John Joseph Dames, of London, England, by his wife, Mary Ann, dau. of James Raysbrook; *b.* London, 20 Nov. 1871; and enlisted in the Sherwood Foresters (Notts and Derby Regt.) in 1885 at the age of 14. In 1897 he was sent to India as Sergeant in charge of a draft for the 2nd Battn., and took part in the Tirah Campaign, receiving the medal. He was at Malta on the way back to England when the Boer War broke out, and at once volunteered for active service; went to South Africa with the Malta Mounted Infantry and served through that campaign. He was twice wounded and was three times mentioned in Dispatches, being awarded the Distinguished Conduct Medal and the Queen's Medal with 3 bars. He was invalided home in 1901, and after being employed as a clerk at the War Office for eight years, went to Canada and settled at Derby town, Alberta. On the outbreak of the European War he again volunteered for active service and enlisted in Princess Patricia's L.I.; came over with the 1st Canadian Contingent; went to France Dec. 1914, and was killed in action at Bellewaarde Lake, near Ypres, 8 May, 1915. Sergt.-Major Dames *m.* at St. George's Church, Stonehouse, Plymouth, 26 July, 1897, Florence (Derbytown, Mound P.O., Alberta, Canada), yst. dau. of the late John Coneybeer, of Ivybridge, co. Devon, and had two sons: Frank Coneybeer, *b.* 15 Sept. 1899; and Harold Victor, *b.* 28 Sept. 1902.

From the Roll of Honour

The Dames Headstone   (PHOTO N. CHRISTIE)

COMPANY-SERGEANT-MAJOR FREDERICK WILLIAM HALL, V.C.

Late 8th Battalion

"On the 24th of April, 1915, in the neighbourhood of Ypres, when a wounded man, who was lying some fifteen yards from the trench, called for help, Company-Sergeant-Major Hall endeavoured to reach him in the face of a very heavy enfilade fire which was being poured in by the enemy. The first attempt failed, and a non-commissioned officer and private soldier, who were attempting to give assistance, were both wounded. Company-Sergeant-Major Hall then made a second most gallant attempt; and was in the act of lifting up the wounded man to bring him in, when he fell mortally wounded in the head."

CAPTAIN (afterwards Lieut.-Colonel) FRANCIS ALEX. CARON SCRIMGER, V.C.

Medical Officer 14th Battalion

"On the afternoon of the 25th of April, 1915, in the neighbourhood of Ypres, when in charge of an advanced dressing station in some farm buildings which were being heavily shelled by the enemy, he directed, under heavy fire, the removal of the wounded, and he himself carried a severely wounded officer out of a stable in search of a place of greater safety. When he was unable alone to carry this officer further, he remained with him under fire till help could be obtained. Captain Scrimger, during the very heavy fighting between the 22nd and 25th of April, displayed continuously, day and night, the greatest devotion to his duty among the wounded at the front."

Victoria Cross Citations Ypres 1915

LANCE-CORPORAL FREDERICK FISHER, V.C.

Late 13th Battalion

"On the 23rd of April, 1915, in the neighbourhood of St. Julien, he went forward with the machine gun of which he was in charge, under heavy fire, and most gallantly assisted in covering the retreat of a battery, losing four men of his gun team. Later, after obtaining four more men, he went forward again to the firing line and was himself killed while bringing his machine gun into action, under very heavy fire, in order to cover the advance of supports."

CAPTAIN EDWARD DONALD BELLEW. V.C.
7th Battalion

"For most conspicuous bravery and devotion to duty near Keerselaere on the 24th of April, 1915, during the German attacks on the Ypres salient, Captain (then Lieutenant) Bellew, as battalion machine-gun officer, had two guns in action on the high ground overlooking Keerselaere. The enemy's attack broke in full force on the morning of the 24th against the front and right flank of the battalion, the latter being exposed owing to a gap in the line. The right company was soon put out of action, but the advance was temporarily stayed by Captain Bellew, who had two of his guns on the left of the right company. Reinforcements were sent forward, but they in turn were surrounded and destroyed. With the enemy in strength less than one hundred yards from him, with no further assistance in sight, and with his rear threatened, Captain Bellew and Sergeant Peerless, each operating a gun, decided to stay where they were and fight it out. Sergeant Peerless was killed and Captain Bellew was wounded and fell. Nevertheless he got up and maintained his fire till ammunition failed and the enemy rushed the position. Captain Bellew then seized a rifle, smashed his machine gun, and, fighting to the last, was taken prisoner."

Victoria Cross Citations Ypres 1915

DUVAL, GEORGE LOUIS JOSIAH, M.D., Major, Commanding No. 1 Coy., Field Ambulance, C.A.M.C., only *s.* of the late Louis Duval, of Grande Ligne, P. Quebec, Canada ; *b.* Grande Ligne aforesaid, 10 March, 1876 ; educ. Filler's Baptist Institute there ; entered as a Medical Student at McGill University in 1894, and

graduated there with honours, 17 June, 1898 ; practised in Waltham, Mass., U.S.A., and then in St. John's, Quebec, later going to St. John's, New Brunswick ; joined the C.A.M.C., at St. John's, P. Quebec, in April, 1908, being given a commission as Lieut., and was promoted Capt. June, 1911, and Major, in France, April, 1915 ; transferred to No. 8 Field Ambulance on going to St. John's, N.B., and in 1914 became M.O. 28th N.B. Dragoons ; volunteered for overseas service on the outbreak of war, and his own unit not going, he was given charge of the section of No. 8 F.A., leaving his home and practice at a day's notice ; left Valcartier for England with No. 1 F.A., 30 Sept. 1914 ; went to France, Feb. 1915, and was severely wounded in both legs during the Second Battle of Ypres, on Sunday, 25 April, 1915. At this action the Canadians suffered heavily, and No. 1 F.A. were

George Louis J. Duval.

ordered to open an advanced dressing station, which Major Duval did at St. Jean ; later it had to be abandoned, and he had just succeeded in evacuating the last patient when he was hit about 8.30 p.m. by an explosive shell which burst about 20 yards from him. He was sent from Vlamertinghe to hospital at Boulogne and from there invalided to England, and died in London, 26 Aug. 1915. Col. Foster wrote : " No braver officer ever lived or would be found in our Division, and I shall always remember him for his slpendid work at Ypres." Gunner H. T. Warene, who was wounded in this action and invalided back to Canada, said : " When I was struck Doctor Duval was the first to rush to my aid. We were both exposed to the fire, but he did not seem to mine. He was a kind, gentle and capable surgeon, and the boys all liked him and admired him as a physician, a soldier, and a man. I was most sorry to learn of his death." He was mentioned in F.M. Sir John (now Lord) French's Despatch of 5 April/31 May [London Gazette, 22 June], 1915. His body was being taken to Canada for burial on board the Hesperian when she was torpedoed and sunk. He *m.* at Montreal, 23 Oct. 1901, Maude (330, Charlotte Street, St. John's West, New Brunswick, Canada), dau. of Andrew Byrd, of Montreal, Building and Bridge Contractor, and had two children : Charles Louis Neville, *b.* 18 July, 1906 ; and Irene Byrd, *b.* 9 Sept. 1902.

BROMLEY, HERBERT ASSHETON (Jett), Lieut., No. 3 Coy., 7th Battn. (1st British Columbia Regt.), Canadian Expeditionary Force, yst. *s.* of the late Sir Henry Bromley, 5th Bt., by his wife, Ada, only child of Westley Richards ; *b.*

Stoke Newark, 16 Oct. 1879 ; educ. Farnborough and Eton, was Private Secretary to his brother, Sir Robert Bromley, Bt., Administrator of St. Christopher and Nevis (1905-6) and afterwards to the Hon. James Dunsmuir, Lieut.-Gov. of British Columbia ; joined the 88th Fusiliers at Victoria, B.C., when that battn. was formed three years ago ; on the outbreak of war volunteered for service overseas, was gazetted Lieut. on formation of Canadian Expeditionary Force, 21 Sept. 1914, and was killed in action at the second Battle of Ypres, 24 April, 1915 ; *unm.* Describing his death, a comrade said : " He was badly wounded in the trenches, but leaped out and led his men in a magnificent charge, calling out ' we have got to win, follow me.' He was quite alone away in front of his men and died a glorious death." His Company Commander, Major R. C. Cooper, wrote to the Editor as follows : " I would, as the late Lieut.

Herbert Assheton Bromley.

H. A. Bromley's Company Commander, like to express my very high appreciation of him, both as an officer with the welfare of his men at heart, and as a personal friend. Mr. Bromley was invaluable to me in France with his intimate knowledge of the language and customs. His men were devoted to him and missed him greatly when wounded in the head on the 16 March at Fleurbaix. He returned to us on 27 March and remained with the battn. up to ' Our Day '—doing duty in the trenches from the 14 to the 19 April, two days in billets and then the gas and subsequent heavy fighting. In Victoria, B.C., he was a member of the 88th Victoria Fusiliers, some time as a Company Officer and the remainder as Adjutant. He served with the regt. in the coal strikes at Nanaimo, Vancouver Island, 1913-14. On the outbreak of war he was one of the first officers selected for Active Service, being posted to my company, left for Valcartier, 28 Aug. 1914, and for England, 27 Sept. 1914, arriving at Plymouth, 15 Oct. 1914—four months of rain at Salisbury Plain and then to France. We all mourn ' Brom.' as a pal and soldier. His last idea, and his was a folorn hope, was to charge and scupper some of the Boches before going under himself. His platoon on 24 April lost twenty-one killed, sixteen wounded, three prisoners and eight wounded and prisoners. This record tells of his work."

CLEARING THE BATTLEFIELDS

The numbers are shocking. The remains of more than 600,000 Commonwealth servicemen lie buried in some 3,500 cemeteries carved quaintly into the rolling hills and farmers' fields of northern France and Belgium.

Landscaped and constructed during the 1920s by the Imperial War Graves Commission (now the Commonwealth War Graves Commission), these cemeteries have frozen the history of the First World War.

The principles of the IWGC, established in 1917 to maintain the cemeteries and record the Commonwealth[3] dead of the Great War (and later the Second World War), were threefold:

1) The name of each serviceman who died in the war or during the immediate postwar would be commemorated on a headstone or engraved on a battlefield memorial.

2) All would receive universal treatment in death.

3) No bodies would be repatriated. All would remain in the country where they died.

The repatriation restriction and the acquisition of the land where the cemeteries originally stood have preserved for perpetuity the legacy left by the hundreds of thousands who sacrificed their lives in foreign lands.

Cemetery Categories

The types of cemeteries fall into three main categories:

1) ***Hospital Centre Cemeteries*** are near main hospital centres or casualty clearing stations. All burials are in chronological order and few graves are unidentified. The officers usually have a separate burial plot, as do Hindus, Moslems and Buddhists. Servicemen of the Jewish faith are usually buried in the Christian plots but there are exceptions. In Étaples, a plot for black soldiers (generally of the British West Indies Regiment) includes one Canadian.

---

[3] The term Commonwealth applies to countries of the old British Empire, namely Australia, New Zealand, India, Pakistan, Canada, South Africa, Britain and other British colonies or protectorates.

2) ***Regimental or Front-Line Cemeteries*** are cemeteries near the front lines for quick burial of soldiers killed at the front (trench wastage) or small battlefield cemeteries set up by Divisional or Corps Burial Officers immediately after a battle. Often the layout and rows are irregular.

3) ***Battlefield Clearance Cemeteries*** were usually small cemeteries greatly expanded after the war by the concentration of remains brought in from surrounding battlefields. They always contain a very high proportion of unidentified graves and the layout of the rows is regular and often symmetric.

Burying the Dead

During the immediate postwar period, the victors faced hundreds of square miles of devastated land, a seemingly infinite amount of war material and munitions and the thousands of isolated graves, both marked and unmarked, scattered throughout the battlefields.

During the war the dead were often buried by their comrades in small regimental cemeteries directly behind the front lines or in cemeteries created near hospitals or Casualty Clearing Stations. For those who fell in the heat of battle, or on territory lost to the Germans, buried by explosions or fallen in areas under constant fire, burial was a rare occurrence. Burial parties made nighttime expeditions into the front line or into No Man's Land where they would place the dead in a shell hole and cover them quickly with a cursory layer of earth. It was a nasty, unpopular and dangerous task and those assigned to the duty would complete it as quickly as possible. The dead were dead. Lists of missing, often presumed dead from the war, ran into the hundreds of thousands. In France and Belgium alone, more than 300,000 are missing or have no known grave.

Throughout the war the Directorate of Grave Registrations and Enquiries (DGRE) in association with Grave Registration Units (GRU) registered each grave, where possible, and established a system to receive all burial reports from Divisional Burial

ANOTHER TRAGEDY

Tragedy befell families throughout Canada during The Great War. Many families lost more than one son, sometimes killed on the same day. But the tragedy that befell the Betts family of Montreal is, perhaps, one of the saddest.

Margaret Bett's 15-year-old son was killed accidentally in Canada in August 1914, while her husband died of a heart attack in England 10 months later. Neither heard a shot fired in anger.

Gordon W. G. Betts.

BETTS, GORDON W. G., Private, 5th Royal Highlanders of Montreal, Canadian Expeditionary Force, only *s.* of the late L.-Corpl. Thomas Henry Betts (who *d.* on active service, 20 June, 1915, see his notice), by his wife, Margaret Jane (121, Prince Arthur Street West, Montreal), dau. of (—) Armitage ; *b.* 16 April, 1899 ; volunteered on the outbreak of war in Aug. 1914, and joined his father's regt., and was accidentally shot, 27 Aug. 1914, while on guard duty at Soulanges Canal, the first Canadian to lose his life on active service in the European War.

Thomas Henry Betts.

BETTS, THOMAS HENRY, L.-Corpl., No. 894, Canadian Army Service Corps, *s.* of Joseph Betts ; *b.* Montreal, 26 Nov. 1870 ; educ. St. Anne's School there ; served for over 20 years with the 5th Royal Highlanders of Montreal, and on the death on service of his son, Private G. W. G. Betts, decided to volunteer for Imperial service, and joined the Canadian A.S.C. in April, 1915. He left for England 13 May following, and *d.* in Newingreen Camp, England, 20 June, 1915, of haemorrhage of the heart. He *m.* at St. Patrick's Church, Montreal, 23 Aug. 1897, Margaret Jane (121, Prince Arthur Street West, Montreal), dau. of (—) Armitage, and had three children : Gordon W. J., *b.* 16 April, 1899, killed on service (see his notice); Helena E. J. and Armitage H. A., *b.* 10 Oct. 1904.

From the Roll of Honour

Officers or chaplains. A master list was kept in London. When the war ended, these records were used to establish a procedure for the battlefield clearances of 1919 through 1921.

The Clearers

After the armistice, Royal Engineer Labor Companies were organized to systematically clear the individual battlefields. The procedures and responsibilities developed for the clearances are outlined below:

1) **The Survey Officer** laid out the area to be searched. He was responsible for instructing the Labor Companies or Exhumation Parties where to conduct the searches and where reburial should take place.

   Land for the permanent war cemeteries was acquired by the DGRE via international agreements with the host countries. Normally, the Survey Officer selected 500-yard squares to be searched and marked the corners with flags. Existing small battlefield cemeteries within the square were marked with blue flags if they contained more than 40 burials and yellow flags if less than 40. The cemeteries were left untouched until specific orders were received to concentrate the burials to a permanent cemetery.

   The Survey Officer also indicated to the officer commanding the exhumations the anticipated number of remains to be found in the area to be searched. This estimate was based on the burial records of the DGRE.

2) **The Army Burial Officer** was in charge of the exhumations. It was his responsibility to ensure the procedures for exhumation were correctly followed and the correct paperwork completed. This responsibility ended when the bodies arrived at the permanent war cemetery.

3) **The Registration Officer** was responsible for the digging parties working inside the permanent war cemeteries. He sanctioned the digging of new graves, the erection of suitable crosses and the completion of the necessary paperwork, correct and in triplicate.

The Exhumation Companies

The principal and most disagreeable task fell to the men of the exhumation companies. Their objective was not only to clear the battlefields for sanitary reasons but to identify the remains often left in shell holes for more than six years! It was essential, therefore, that the area being searched was done so systematically and carefully. The men were assured their work was of vital importance in determining the fate of the large number of men who, in 1919, 1920 and 1921, were still listed as missing. Many could be found and identified by the exhumation companies if the work was done carefully.

The exhumation company was organized into squads of 32 men and subdivided into squads of four. Each squad was supplied with a 500-square-yard map (already surveyed and designated by the Survey Officer), two pairs of rubber gloves, two shovels, stakes to mark the locations of graves found, canvas and rope to tie up remains, stretchers, cresol (a poisonous colorless isomeric phenol) and wire cutters.

The officer in charge had a map of the area (1:20,000 scale), labels to attach to the bodies, ration bags for recovered personal effects and a notebook. All remains, whether Allied or German, were to be removed from the battlefield and concentrated into a permanent war cemetery.

The search would start in the 500-yard square. The men were instructed not to bunch and to span the ground slowly, placing a stake where remains were found. After a thorough search, they would return to each stake and exhume the remains. When the graves were unmarked, experience was the only method of knowing where to dig. However, characteristic signs were as follows:

i)   rifles or stakes protruding from the ground, bearing helmets or equipment;

ii) partial remains or equipment on the surface or protruding from the ground;

iii) rat holes — often small bones or pieces of equipment will be brought to the surface by the rats;

CAMERON, DONALD EWAN, of Montreal, Quebec, Canada, Lieut., Princess Patricia's Canadian L.I., yst. *s.* of the late Archibald Cameron, Manager of the Merchants' Bank of Canada, Toronto, by his wife, Agnes Margaret, dau. of Major

James Barwick, 79th Cameron Highlanders, and grandson of Lieut.-Col. Duncan Cameron, C.B., 79th Cameron Highlanders (who fought at Waterloo); *b.* Toronto, 18 Dec. 1870; educ. Trinity College School, Port Hope, and the Montreal High School, and on leaving school entered the service of the Canadian Bank of Commerce. In 1902 he formed the Lilley and Cameron Cartage Co., and later the Terminal Warehouse & Cartage Co. of Montreal. In 1912 he became associated with the Dominion Securities Corporation. He served in the Canadian Militia for many years— first in the Victoria Rifles of Canada, then in all the ranks up to that of Major in the Duke of York's Royal Canadian Hussars, and went on the Reserve of Officers. He joined the Princess Patricia's Canadian L.I. upon the organisation of the regt. for service in Aug. 1914; sailed with the Canadian Contingent in Oct.; was encamped on Salisbury Plain and at Winchester, and left for France on 20 Dec. 1914.

Donald Ewan Cameron.

The regt. was sent up to the trenches in the neighbourhood of Ypres, and was constantly engaged. He fell in the counter-attack upon the Germans at St. Eloi, 15 March, 1915, and was buried in the Princess Patricia's Canadian L.I. cemetery at Voormezeele; *unm.* His brother, Col. Kenneth Cameron, of Montreal, was the officer in charge of the Surgical Division of No. 1 Canadian General Hospital at Netheravon on Salisbury Plain, and Etaples, France, and later officer commanding No. 2 Canadian General Hospital at Le Tréport, France.

BINGHAM, CHARLES JEFFREY SLADE, Private, No. 20745, 10th Battn. Canadian Expeditionary Force, 3rd *s.* of the late Richard Charles William Bingham, of Bingham's Melcombe, co. Dorset, J.P., Lieut.-Col., Dorsetshire Regt., by his wife, Georgina (28ᴀ, Barons Court Road, West Kensington), dau. of William Stuckey Wood, of Charlton Musgrove, Wincanton, late Capt. 7th Dragoon Guards, and grandson of Col. Charles Bingham, Royal Artillery Dep. Adj.-Gen.; *b.* Bingham's Melcombe, co. Dorset, 12 Dec. 1893, and was educ. at Clifton College, from which he went to Canada in 1910, and at the outbreak of the war joined the 10th Battn. Canadian Expeditionary Force. While in camp at Valcartier he contracted cerebro-spinal meningitis and was landed at Plymouth on 15 Oct. 1914, in a very serious condition, and taken to the 4th Southern Military

Charles Jeffrey Slade Bingham.

Hospital, where he died on 6 Jan. 1915; *unm.* Four of his brothers are now (1916) on active service, Richard Charles Otho with the Ceylon Engineers in Ceylon; John Richard, 2nd Lieut., R.F.C., late H.A.C.; Humphrey Richard, Lieut., R.F.A. (awarded the Military Cross, in Jan. 1915); and William Philip, 2nd Lieut., R.F.C., all with the Expeditionary Force in France

CAMERON, EVAN STUART, Corpl., No. 25931 (Royal Montreal Regt.), 14th Battn. Canadian Expeditionary Force, eldest surviving *s.* of Sir Edward John Cameron, K.C.M.G., Governor and Commander-in-Chief of Gambia, by his wife, Eva Selwyn, dau. of the late Robert Mackintosh Isaacs,

LL.D., of New South Wales; *b.* Turks Island, West Indies, 21 Sept. 1893; educ. Blundell's School, Tiverton (1905-12), where he was head for two years, and on leaving there in Sept. 1912, went to Montreal to join the Royal Bank of Canada. He enlisted in the Canadian Contingent on the outbreak of war, Aug. 1914, and was killed in action near St. Julien, 24 April, 1915; *unm.* Major Beatty, A.D.C. to General Alderson, Commanding 1st Canadian Contingent, wrote: "He was dearly loved by all his comrades, and he had earned the respect and admiration of all, and had behaved with the greatest gallantry all through that dreadful time from 5 p.m. on Thursday, 22 April, up to the time of his death." His Capt. said: "He handled his men wonderfully, and would have been given a commission had he survived the battle," and the head master of Blundells: "As I look back upon his school career I feel that we have lost one of the most sterling of the old pupils

Evan Stuart Cameron.

whom I remember in my long experience of 40 years." He was a good cricketer, and was capt. of the cricket eleven and football fifteen for two years at Blundells and won the average bat four years in succession. He played against the Australian XI in 1913 and made the first century of the season for the McGill Cricket Club in July, 1914. He also played at Lords in 1912 in a Public Schools XI.

iv)   discoloration of grass, earth or water — grass was often a vivid bluish-green with broader blades where bodies were buried, while earth and water turned a greenish-black or grey color;

Generally, many more remains than DGRE documents indicated were found. Once the area had been searched, they would commence the task of exhumation.

A Nauseating Experience

In 1919, this task was most unpleasant as much of the corpse remained, and were quite repulsive to touch. Identifying corpses whose identification discs had been driven into the flesh by a projectile was also a considerable problem. By 1921 decomposition made the task less disagreeable.

The exhumation squad would dig gently around the stake (in case more than one body was buried) and place the body or bodies on cresol-soaked canvas. For identification purposes, a careful examination of pockets, the neck, wrists and braces (places where soldiers often kept their identification tags) was required. All personal effects would be placed in a ration bag. The body would be wrapped in the canvas and tied.

The ration bag and tag (listing map reference, name, unit, list of effects found, etc. and cemetery to be reburied) would be attached to the canvas. Only the officer-in-charge was permitted to complete this label.

He would also indicate on the tag whether a committal service was necessary, depending on whether he believed the body had previously been properly committed. Remains were then placed on a transport wagon or in a field ambulance and taken to a permanent war cemetery, accompanied by the original cross if any.

Once the body had been removed from the grave, any equipment not required for identification was returned to the grave, the ground treated with cresol and the grave filled. If more than one body was found in a grave the remains were kept together so they could be reburied together in a permanent cemetery. This was done to allow future identification should additional records shed light on the burials.

13. LONGUEVAL Cemetery

Clearing the Battlefield. The Exhumation Company at Work — The Somme 1919.)

The Flyers

The local people who had fled their homes and farms in the battle-torn areas of France and Belgium returned quickly after the war. During reconstruction of the villages, remains found were recovered by the exhumation company's "Flying Squads." The transport proceeded to a designated permanent cemetery where the Registration Officer and the cemetery party took control.

At the Permanent War Cemetery

The party at the permanent war cemetery comprised the registration officer, a chaplain, a digging party of the 20 men and a sanitary man. The cemetery was laid out in advance, subdivided into plots and rows and a 40-foot trench, 4.5 feet deep, hollowed out. When the transport arrived, the remains were interred in pre-selected locations and any original crosses were placed at the head of the graves. If there was no cross, a GRU cross with stamped aluminum identification strip was erected.

The Effects Branch

At this point the personal effects were reexamined for identification and then forwarded to the Effects Branch at the Base. The graves were filled and the chaplain read the burial service over the remains (if necessary). If German prisoner-of-war labor was used for digging the graves, the POWS were removed from the cemetery for the committal service.

The stretchers were washed with cresol and returned to the exhumation parties. During working hours visitors were not admitted to the cemetery.

Between 1919 and 1921, 200,000 concentrations took place in France and Belgium. Less than half were identified.

Completion

Throughout the 1920s, the permanent war cemeteries you see today were constructed and landscaped. The burial mounds were leveled and headstones replaced the wooden crosses.

Nearly eight decades on, the maintenance of these war graves is big business! The operating budget for the Commonwealth War Graves Commission, which is based in England and has offices in France, Belgium and Italy, is approximately $60,000,000 (1995). Canada pays for 10 per cent of this.

The grave of a serviceman can be traced through the CWGC offices. "Cemetery overprint" Michelin maps can also be obtained from its offices in Maidenhead, England; Arras, France; Ypres, Belgium; and Rome, Italy. Map Numbers 51, 52 and 53 cover the Western Front. Map 51 covers the Ypres Salient (1:200,000).

INNES HOPKINS, CASTELL PERCY, Private, 9th (Service) Battn. Gordon Highlanders, 2nd *s.* of Lieut.-Col. Charles Harrie Innes Hopkins, of The Towers, Ryton-on-Tyne, late 2nd Scottish Rifles, now commanding the 1st Tyneside Scottish, by his wife, Helen Elizabeth, dau. of the late Gen. Sir Thomas Edward Gordon, K.C.B., K.C.I.E., C.S.I.; *b.* Naini Tal, N.W.P., India, 31 July, 1889; educ. Dunchurch Hall, and Fribourg, Germany, afterwards being employed in his father's offices in Newcastle. On the outbreak of war he enlisted in the 9th Battn. Gordon Highlanders, and left with his regt. for the Front, May, 1915, and fell in action during the charge on Hill 70 at Loos, 25 Sept. 1915; *unm.* His elder brother, John Gordon Innes Hopkins, is now (1916) serving in the Naval Brigade, having travelled specially from Japan, where he was in the R.M.S.P. Co. when the war broke out, to join the Navy as a volunteer, and his yr. brother, Lieut. C. R. Innes Hopkins, 2nd Scottish Rifles, and his uncle, Capt. James Randolph Innes Hopkins, Canadian Expeditionary Force, were both killed in action (see their notices).

INNES HOPKINS, CHARLES RANDOLPH, Lieut., 2nd Battn. The Cameronians (Scottish Rifles), 3rd *s.* (see previous notice) of Lieut.-Col. Charles Harrie Innes Hopkins, of The Towers, Ryton-on-Tyne, late 2nd Scottish Rifles, now

commanding the 1st Tyneside Scottish, by his wife, Helen Elizabeth, dau. of the late Gen. Sir Thomas Edward Gordon, K.C.B., K.C.I.E., C.S.I.; *b.* Ranikhet, N.W.P., India, 9 Aug. 1893; educ. Dunchurch Hall, Uppingham (scholar), and Sandhurst, where he gained the prize for military law and passed out the second term "third" with honours; gazetted 2nd Lieut., 2nd Battn. Scottish Rifles, 4 Sept. 1912, and promoted Lieut., 24 Oct. 1913; was in Malta with his regt. when war broke out; they returned to England, and went to the Front, 4 Nov. 1914, and he was killed in action in the trenches at Neuve Chapelle, France, 18 Dec. 1914; *unm.* Buried in the orchard of the farm behind Neuve Chapelle. His company officer wrote: "I would like to say how very greatly I have valued his presence, from the day he joined. He has always been my subaltern and a very close companion to me.

Charles R. Innes Hopkins.

In all things I have trusted him implicitly, and in all things he has proved himself worthy. I know that he was good in thought, and word, and deed—that he could not do a wrong thing—that he would not lose heart, and that he was the loyalist subaltern and the finest friend that ever man had. We all feel his loss very deeply, especially his men." A writer in the "Newcastle Journal" (23 Dec. 1914) said: "Of Charles Hopkins it could be truly said that he was one of Nature's most perfect gentlemen, and if ever anyone seemed destined for a great future it was he. As able and gifted as he was modest, possessed of strong purpose, exceptional talents, sound judgment, and a personality infinitely attractive, there seemed to be nothing he could not have achieved had he tried. An excellent cricketer and hockey player, an expert ski-er, a 'crack' shot, and fine billiard player, there was no sport at which he did not excel, whilst in classics, military law and tactics he came out with highest honours. He had a soldier's love and pride in his work, and if genius, as has been said, is an infinite capacity for taking pains, his career, had he been spared, would have proved him a soldier of genius."

INNES HOPKINS, JAMES RANDOLPH, Capt., 5th Battn. 2nd Infantry Brigade, Canadian Expeditionary Force, yst.

s. of William Randolph Innes Hopkins, of The Leat, Malton, by his wife, Evereld Catherine Eliza, dau. of Thomas Hustler; *b.* at Grey Towers, Cleveland, 5 Oct. 1876; educ. at Aysgarth, Yorks, and Oriel College, Oxford; served in the South African War, 1899-1902, as a trooper and was afterwards given a commission in the Northumberland Hussars; went to Canada in 1906, and settled in Saskatchewan. On the outbreak of the European War in Aug. 1914, he immediately offered his services and was given a commission as Capt. 22 Sept. following; came over with the first contingent in Oct.; was stationed on Salisbury Plain during the winter, 1914-15; went to France in Feb., and was killed in action at Neuve Chapelle, 24 May, 1915, while leading his men. Capt. Hopkins' two nephews, Private C. P. Innes Hopkins and Lieut. C. R. Innes Hopkins, were both killed in action (see their notices). He

James R. Innes Hopkins.

m. in London, 29 Sept. 1904, Doreen Maud (who *m.* secondly, 6 Oct. 1915, Thomas Sackville Manning), eldest dau. of the Hon. Reginald Parker [6th *s.* of Thomas, 6th Earl of Macclesfield], and had a dau., Evereld, *b.* 1905.

CEMETERIES AND MEMORIALS

Most of the 2,000 Canadians who died at the Second Battle of Ypres were never found or identified. In April 1915, there was no identification tag system and many soldiers had no identification on them at all. Others had their personal effects or aluminum ID bracelets removed by the Germans, so when the battlefields were cleared in 1919, no identification remained on the bodies.

The Germans who had taken the battlefield did not take care in burying the dead. For hygienic reasons, they disposed of the remains as quickly as possible. The fighting over this terrain in 1917 also resulted in the destruction of graves. Still green and flush in 1915, the Ypres Salient became a quagmire during the Third Battle of Ypres, July to November 1917.

Nonetheless, when the time came to clear the battlefields, isolated graves of soldiers or groups of soldiers were found, as well as the Fields of Honour made by the Germans near Poelcappelle. The remains of these graves were brought to Permanent War Cemeteries for burial. Unfortunately, most were unidentified. Only the graves of soldiers who died of wounds or as prisoners of war are identified. These are the main cemeteries containing graves of Canadian soldiers who died at Ypres.

THE MENIN GATE MEMORIAL

The Menin Gate Memorial, on the eastern edge of the old town on the Ypres-Menin road, is a Memorial to the Missing or to soldiers who died in the Ypres Salient and have no known grave. It is the principal place for the commemoration of soldiers who died in the Second Battle of Ypres.

Engraved on its walls are the names of 55,000 Commonwealth soldiers who died in the salient and have no known grave. Of the names, 6,983 are those of Canadians who predominantly were missing after the battles of Ypres 1915 (roughly 1,200), St. Eloi 1916, Mount Sorrel 1916 and Passchendaele 1917. The name panels are arranged by unit.

The Menin Gate

At the top of the 4th Canadian Infantry panel is Lieutenant Colonel Arthur Birchall, the commanding officer killed near Turco Farm on Mauser Ridge. Near the top of the list for Canadian Field Artillery is Lieutenant A. H. Helmer, whose death inspired his friend John MacCrae to write the poem, In Flanders Fields. On the panel of the 8th Canadian Infantry is Company Sergeant Major F. W. Hall, VC, who died helping wounded comrades. On the 13th Canadian panel is Lance Corporal Frederick Fisher, VC, who died valiantly covering the open flank just north of the Ypres-Poelcappelle road and west of Poelcappelle on April 24, 1915.

Designed by Sir Reginald Bloomfield, the memorial was unveiled in 1927. Every night at 8 p.m., traffic on both sides of the memorial comes to a halt while buglers of the Ypres Fire Brigade sound The Last Post. This is a very moving experience.

Not all ex-soldiers thought such a memorial was in good taste. The famous First World War poet, Siegfried Sassoon, wrote a poem, *On Passing the New Menin Gate,* in which he expresses his disgust with the monument.

ON PASSING THE NEW MENIN GATE

Who will remember, passing through this Gate,
The unheroic Dead who fed the guns?
Who shall absolve the foulness of their fate —
Those doomed, conscripted, unvictorious ones?
    Crudely renewed, the Salient holds it own.
    Paid are its dim defenders by this pomp;
    Paid, with a pile of peace-complacent stone,
    The Armies who endured that sullen swamp.

Here was the world's worst wound. And here with pride
'Their name liveth for ever' the Gateway claims.
Was ever an immolation so belied
As these intolerably nameless names?
Well might the Dead who struggled in the slime
Rise and deride this sepulchre of crime.

Siegfried Sassoon

(PHOTO N. CHRISTIE)

Poelcapelle British Cemetery

POELCAPPELLE BRITISH CEMETERY

Poelcappelle is nine kilometres northeast of Ypres. The cemetery lies in open country east of the village on the road to Westrozebeke and was made in 1919 and 1920 from the clearances of the battlefields of Ypres and Passchendaele.

It contains the graves of 7,469 Commonwealth soldiers, 83 per cent unidentified, and mainly soldiers killed in the Battle of Third Ypres in 1917. Of the 525 Canadians in the cemetery, 417 (80 per cent) are unidentified. One hundred and sixteen of the Canadians were killed at Ypres in 1915, most of them unidentified and principally from the 13th, 14th and 15th Battalions. They were killed closing the open flank April 22 to 24, 1915. In fact, only 13 are identified. Plot 49, Row E, Grave 12 contains the remains of an unknown captain of the Royal Montreal Regiment (14th Battalion). He is, probably, Captain R. Steacie, killed April 22 at St. Julien.

During the clearances, members of the 48th Labour Company started a fire to cook their midday meal, right over a buried, unexploded, high explosive shell. Seven men were killed outright and are buried in Plot 17, Row C, Graves 11 to 17.

This cemetery is perhaps the one that most represents the salient. The high percentage of unknowns illustrates more than anything the grotesque horrors that occurred near Ypres between 1914 and 1917. An atmosphere of despair lingers here, of souls lost in the quagmire of Ypres. As it is not near Ypres itself, it receives few visitors.

TYNE COT BRITISH CEMETERY

Three kilometre southwest of Passchendaele village, Tyne Cot British Cemetery is the largest Commonwealth War Cemetery in the world. It was enlarged after the war, between 1919 and 1921, but the cemetery's original burials are just north of the Cross of Sacrifice. Here lie the graves of 11,871 Commonwealth soldiers, of which 8,365 (70 per cent) are unidentified.

Of the 966 Canadians buried in this cemetery, 554 are unknown. Sixty-four of the Canadians here were killed in the Second Battle of Ypres. Only 11 of them are identified. Most of

WALLACE, HENRY ATHOLL CHARLES, Capt., 10th Battn. 2nd Brigade, Canadian Expeditionary Force, eldest *s.* of the late Henry Wallace, of Trench

Hall, co. Durham, J.P., for many years Agent to the Earl of Ravensworth ; by his wife, Jessie (139, Ware Road, Hertford), dau. of Charles Ellis, of New York, U.S.A. ; *b.* Trench Hall, Gateshead-on-Tyne, 1879 ; educ. Uppingham College ; served in the South African War with the Northumberland Imperial Yeomanry, 1900-1901 (Queen's medal with two clasps) ; emigrated to Canada in 1902, and after farming in Manitoba for a short time, turned his attention to real estate ; joined the 106th Winnipeg L.I. in Winnipeg, Canada ; volunteered for Imperial service on the outbreak of war and was appointed Capt. 10th Battn. (Winnipeg L.I.) ; came over with the 1st Contingent in Oct. 1914 ; trained on Salisbury Plain during the winter ; went to France early in Feb. and after serving in the trenches for two months, was killed in action at Langemarck, 22 April, 1915. He always took a keen interest in military matters, and belonged in Canada to the Veterans' Brigade, composed of men who had served their

Henry A. C. Wallace.

country in any part of the world. He *m.* at St. Mary's, Gateshead-on-Tyne, 1903, Winifred (194, Hill Street, Norwood Road, Winnipeg, Manitoba, Canada), dau. of the late Thomas Archer, of the Dunston Engine Works, Dunston-on-Tyne, a well-known engineer and inventor, and had two children : Henry Archer Harold, *b.* 3 April, 1906 ; and Dorothy Laura, *b.* 15 March, 1909.

LIPSETT, WILLIAM ALFRED, Barrister-at-Law, Private, No. 20330, 10th Battn. Canadian Infantry, yst. *s.* of the late Robert Lipsett, Ballyshannon, Ireland ; *b.* at Ballyshannon, 29 Jan. 1886 ; educ. St. Andrew's College, Dublin, and

Trinity College, Dublin. He was a member of the Irish Bar, but in the spring of 1914 went out to Canada and was engaged in legal work in Calgary, Alberta. Two days after war broke out he volunteered, enlisting as a private, and refusing a commission. He came home with the 1st Canadian Contingent, and went to France with them in Feb. 1915. He was killed on the night of 22-23 April, 1915, at the Second Battle of Ypres during the charge of the 10th and 16th Canadian Battns. on the wood to the west of St. Julien. It will be remembered that these regts. charged through the wood, against far superior numbers, under the heaviest machine-gun fire, and actually reached a point 500 yards in advance of the wood, retaking the four British guns which had been lost in the afternoon of 22 April. Unfortunately the casualties were very high. The 10th Battn. went into the wood 1,000 strong, and came out only 200 strong.

William Alfred Lipsett.

Mr. Lipsett played a gallant part in this attack. As Major Ormond, who took over command of the 10th Battn. after Col. Boyle was killed, wrote : " I saw Lipsett the night that he was killed ; we went into action charging the wood west of St. Julien at 11.50 p.m., April 22. The Grenadiers were grouped on our left flank and did exceptionally well, Lipsett being one of them. As soon as we had taken the trench, they continued along to the left until they were stopped. Lipsett like the others was very cool and appeared to have no fear. They were subject to the most severe machine-gun fire I have known, but pressed on until all were killed and wounded. I regret to say that as he was killed within 10 or 15 yards from the German redoubt at the corner of the wood we were unable to recover his body. He was an excellent soldier." His Adjutant also wrote : " He was a gallant soldier and is deeply regretted by all ranks," and again, " He rendered valuable service to his Battn. and is universally regretted." His eldest brother, Captain Lewis R. Lipsett, also a member of the Irish Bar, is (1916) serving in the Army Service Corps, with the Expeditionary Force in France. His cousin, Brigadier-General Lewis J. Lipsett, formerly of the Royal Irish Regt., was appointed a C.M.G. for his services at the Second Battle of Ypres, while in command of the 8th Battn. Canadian Infantry.

the other burials are Canadians killed in the Passchendaele fighting of 1917.

In 1920, during the clearances near St. Julien, the Labour Company found a cross marked "Unknown Canadian Officer — Royal Highlanders of Canada." During exhumation, they found two unknown officers and four soldiers, and concluded by the length of the femur that one officer was about 6'3 or 6'4". A reference to archives records ascertained the officer was Lieutenant Guy Drummond of the 13th Battalion, who had been buried with Major E. C. Norsworthy. Thus, both sets of remains were identified. The four soldiers found with them remain unidentified.

This group was among the soldiers who raced to fill the gap left by the fleeing French forces and who, against the impossible odds, stood against the oncoming Germans. Norsworthy and Drummond are buried in Plot 59, Row B, Graves 24 and 28.

The cemetery also contains a memorial to 34,000 British soldiers who died in the Ypres Salient after August 15, 1917 and have no known grave, and 1,150 New Zealanders killed in the Battle of Passchendaele 1917 and have no known graves.

PERTH (CHINA WALL) CEMETERY, ZILLEBEKE

Perth Cemetery is on the road between Ypres and Zillebeke, three kilometres east of the town. It was enlarged in 1919 and 1920 and again between 1924 and 1925 by battlefield clearances over a wide area.

The number of remains discovered in the salient exceeded original expectations and, as cemeteries became filled, space had to be found in open cemeteries. This is why many soldiers are buried some distance from where they fell. In addition, for about 15 years after the end of the war, at least a thousand sets of remains were discovered annually and reburied in open cemeteries, often some distance from where they were found.

In 1924 and 1925, five small cemeteries made by the Germans after the fighting of 1915 were concentrated into this cemetery.

Those cemeteries were:

St. Julien Communal Cemetery, contained six men of the 14th Battalion.

St. Julien East German Military Cemetery, at the foot of the Gravenstafel Ridge where the 7th Battalion made their stand on April 24, 1915 and where Bellew won his VC, contained predominantly 7th Battalion soldiers

Wallenolen Cemetery of Honour, 500 metres south at Poelcappelle village, contained soldiers of the 13th and 15th Battalions

Poelcappelle Cemetery of Honour, No. 2 and No. 3, 500 metres south of Poelcappelle village, contained men of the 13th and 15th Battalions

Perth Cemetery contains 2,763 Commonwealth graves of which 1,368 (50 per cent) are unidentified. Of the 133 Canadian burials, 77 are unidentified. From the Second Battle of Ypres are 77 Canadian dead, only 12 of which are identified.

RAILWAY DUGOUTS (TRANSPORT FARM) BURIAL GROUND, ZILLEBEKE

Three kilometres from Ypres en route to Zillebeke, this cemetery was made during the war and enlarged by the clearances in 1924.

It contains 2,029 Commonwealth war dead including 430 unknowns. There are 636 Canadians in the cemetery, the majority of whom were killed holding the line near Zillebeke in 1916.

They are mostly original burials, but in 1924 a number of isolated graves were brought in as well as the remains from a large mass grave undoubtedly dug by the Germans. It contained 40 soldiers, predominantly men of the 2nd, 3rd and 16th Battalions, killed northwest of Kitcheners Wood on April 22 and 23, 1915. Only four are identified. They are now buried in Plot 8.

OOSTTAVERNE WOOD CEMETERY

The cemetery, south of St. Eloi on the road to Rijsel (Lille), was created predominantly by battlefield clearances in 1926. The majority of the soldiers buried here were found in unmarked isolated graves.

JESSOP, NAPIER ARNOTT, Lieut., 7th Battn. (1st British Columbia Regt.) Canadian Expeditionary Force, only *s.* of the late George Henry Jessop, of Crediton, Devonshire, by his wife, Ethel Marian, only dau. of the late John Frederick Bell, Capt. Loyal North Lancashire Regt. ; *b.* Taunton, co. Somerset, 28 May, 1889 ; educ. private school at Bishop's Stortford ; went to Vancouver Island, British Columbia, in 1908, where he was first farming, and later went into real estate business, received a commission as Lieut. in 88th Victoria Fusiliers, 16 Sept. 1912, and served with them on strike duty at Nanaimo, B.C., from Aug. 1913 until the outbreak of war ; appointed Lieut. in 7th Battn, Canadian Expeditionary Force, 22 Sept. 1914 ; came over with the first contingent in Oct. 1914 ; left for France, 10 Feb. 1915, and was killed in action near St. Julien during the heroic stand of the Canadians in the 2nd Battle of Ypres, 24 April, 1915 ; *unm.* His Commanding Officer wrote : " Lieut. Jessop was on the right of our battn. line, the section

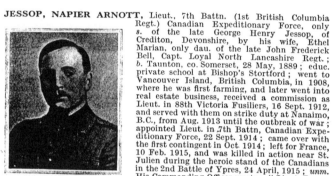

Napier Arnott Jessop.

which was first surrounded, and which was later practically wiped out. Lieut. Jessop, all agree, was perfectly splendid under the fierce attack that was thrown against us that day. He was an inspiration to his men. There is not much to tell, for his platoon were in trenches throughout, and merely fought the Germans off by rifle fire. There was nothing spectacular about it, but it was the height of enduring courage."

The cemetery contains 1,119 Commonwealth graves of which 783 (70 per cent) are unknown. Of those, 133 are Canadian soldiers killed in Ypres in 1915. Twenty-three come from a mass grave found in 1926 at the western toe of the Gravenstafel Ridge. They are mostly from the 7th Battalion, killed defending the ridge on April 24. Among the dead is Lieutenant Napier Jessop and another unknown lieutenant, both of the 7th, killed when Bellew won his VC. They are buried in Plots 5 and 6, Rows G and H.

NEW IRISH FARM CEMETERY

The cemetery is on the left side of the Ypres-Roulers (Poelcappelle) highway four kilometres northwest of Ypres in an open field. The cemetery was initiated in 1917, but after the war more than 4,500 graves were brought in from battlefield clearances. It contains 4,678 Commonwealth soldiers of which 3,267 are unknown (70 per cent).

It contains 254 soldiers from Canada, 60 of whom were killed on Mauser Ridge or near Kitcheners Wood. They were found singly in isolated graves.

BEDFORD HOUSE CEMETERY ENCLOSURES NO. 4 AND 6

The cemetery is found on the road to Rijsel, three kilometres north of Oosttaverne Wood Cemetery.

It was used throughout the war and, later, remains were brought into it from the battlefield clearances.

Enclosure No. 4 contains the graves of 3,475 Commonwealth soldiers including 309 Canadians. Only six (all unknown) are associated with the Second Battle of Ypres and all were found between 1921 and 22 in isolated graves.

Enclosure No. 6 was for remains recovered by farmers between 1932 and 1939. It contains 54 Canadians, 12 of whom were found in the battlefield of Ypres 1915. It also contains the remains of five men from the 7th and 14th Battalions found in a mass grave in St. Julien in 1938. All are unknown.

FURTHER AFIELD

To the West

POPERINGHE OLD MILITARY CEMETERY

The cemetery is on the south side of Poperinghe, a town 10 kilometres due west of Ypres. It was used between October 1914 and May 1915 and contains 444 graves of which 48 are Canadian. All the Canadians here died as a result of the Battle of Ypres.

Two of the burials are Commanding Officers. Buried in Plot 2, Row M, Grave 54 is Lieutenant Colonel Russ Boyle of the 10th Battalion (Alberta), who died April 25, 1915, of wounds received at Kitchener's Wood. Buried in Plot 2, Row M, Grave 3 is Lieutenant Colonel William Hart-McHarg, commander of the 7th Battalion (British Columbia) who died April 24, 1915, of wounds received near Keerselaere.

BOULOGNE EASTERN CEMETERY, FRANCE

Boulogne is 100 kilometres west of Ypres on the English Channel coast. The cemetery was used from 1914 to 1918 and contains 442 Canadian burials. Due to soil conditions, the headstones lie flat. A hospital centre throughout the war, Boulogne is typical of many hospital centre cemeteries. The officers are separated from the other ranks and the men are buried in chronological order, three to a grave, and there are few unknowns.

Of the 442 Canadians, 52 succumbed to wounds received in the Second Battle of Ypres. Of interest is the grave of Captain Frederick W. Campbell, VC, of the 1st Canadian Battalion (Western Ontario). Campbell won his Victoria Cross for bravery in the Battle of Givenchy in June 1915. He was severely wounded in the action and died four days later.

Sadly, many Second Battle of Ypres survivors, like Campbell, would fine a grave at Festubert or Givenchy in May and June 1915. This year marked the end of the 1st Contingent, the originals.

There are also several plots containing the remains of Commonwealth servicemen killed in the Second World War, including several Canadians killed at Dieppe.

To the East:

ROULERS COMMUNAL CEMETERY

Roulers is 23 kilometres east of Ypres. The cemetery is in the western part of the town. It contains 88 Commonwealth graves, including 24 Canadians. All died as prisoners-of-war; 23 were wounded and captured at the Second Battle of Ypres.

This tour has concentrated solely on the actions of the Canadians in the Second Battle of Ypres, April 1915. However, the infamous reputation of Ypres far exceeded that battle. The Ypres Salient, the largest burial ground in the world, would claim thousands more Canadians at Mount Sorrel in 1916 and Passchendaele in 1917.

The monuments and cemeteries of the British, Australians, New Zealanders, French, Belgian and Germans are densely scattered throughout the old salient and deserve a visit.

SCOTT, FRANCIS WILLIAM, Sapper, No. 5203, Canadian Engineers, Canadian Expeditionary Force, late Lieut., R.N., yr. *s.* of the late Hon. Henry Robert Hepburne-Scott, of Knipton, Grantham,

by his wife, Lady Ada, née Douglas Home (Nisbet Mill, Ancrum, Roxburghshire), dau. of Cospatrick, 11th Earl of Home ; *b.* Springhill, Coldstream, 19 Aug. 1886 ; educ. Remenham, Henley - on - Thames, and Ascham School, Bournemouth ; entered the Royal Navy as a Naval Cadet on H.M.S. Britannia, 24 May, 1901, became Sub-Lieut., March, 1907, and Lieut., 31 Dec. 1908 ; and was invalided out of the service in Aug. 1912, owing to deafness. He then went to British Columbia and when war broke out was at Kitselas, on the Skeener River, Prince Rupert. He immediately went to Vancouver City and joined the 1st Coy. Canadian Engineers. He came over with the first contingent, Oct. 1914 ; went to France, Feb. 1915, and died, 4 May, 1915, in Boulogne Hospital, from wounds received in action on the Ypres Canal two days previously. He was buried in the British Military Division, Boulogne Cemetery (Grave No. 1885) ; *unm.* He received

Francis William Scott.

the bronze medal of the Royal Humane Society for saving life at sea, 15 Jan. 1910, while acting as Lieut. on H.M.S. Hindustan off Spithead.

CAMERON, MORTON AUGUSTUS, Private, No. 22557, 15th Battn. (48th Highlanders of Canada), Canadian Expeditionary Force, only *s.* of Augustus Morton Cameron, of St. Stephen's, New Brunswick, Canada, Labourer, by his wife, Isabella Mary, dau. of Caleb Hennessey ; *b.* St. Stephen's

afsd. 27 Nov. 1896 ; educ. Mark Street School there ; volunteered on the outbreak of war and enlisted in the 71st New Brunswick Regt. at St. Stephen's, 8 Aug. 1914. After 3 weeks at Fredericton, N.B., he was sent to Valcartier, where he was transferred to the 12th Battn., and left for England with the first Canadian contingent. They landed at Plymouth on 14 Oct. and trained on Salisbury Plain during the winter of 1914-15. On 23 April, 1915, he was transferred to the 15th Battn., and went over to France with a draft for that Battn. and joined it in the trenches at Ypres. He went through the fighting at Ploegsteert Wood and Festubert, and was killed in action

Morton Augustus Cameron.

at Messines, 10 Nov. 1915 ; *unm.* He was buried in the Military Cemetery near Ration Hill. His captain wrote that he had been sent out with a party to repair the front trench, and that a piece of shell hit him on the head killing him almost instantaneously.

HOPLEY, HERBERT, Private, No. 27352, 15th Battn. (48th Highlanders of Canada), Canadian Expeditionary Force, *s.* of Stephen Hopley, of 35, Bloomsbury Road, Ramsgate, by

his wife, Mary Ann, dau. of William Willmott, of Ramsgate ; *b.* Ramsgate, 15 May, 1888 ; educ. Christ Church School, Ramsgate, and worked for eight years for Tucker & Son, Smack Owners and Sail Makers ; went to Canada about 1912, and was for two years in the employ of J. J. Turner & Sons, Tent Makers, Peterborough, Ontario, after which he went to Toronto ; volunteered on the outbreak of war and joined the Canadian Expeditionary Force in Aug. 1914 ; left Valcartier Camp for England in Oct. 1914 ; trained on Salisbury Plain during the winter of 1914-15 ; went to France, Feb. 1915, and died of gas poisoning at the Battle of St. Julien 26 April, 1915 ; *unm.*

Herbert Hopley.

IN FLANDERS FIELDS

The classic poem of The Great War, *In Flanders Fields*, was written by a Canadian Army Medical Corps officer in May 1915.

John McCrae penned the verse near Essex Farm, along the Ypres Canal north of Ypres after a week of shocking action. Although a veteran of the Boer War, McCrae would have seen nothing like the suffering that went on at the Second Battle of Ypres.

On the morning of May 2, a German heavy shell burst in the Canadian artillery positions on the banks of the Ypres Canal, killing instantly McCrae's good friend Lieutenant Alexis Helmer of Ottawa. Lieutenant Owen Hague of Montreal was mortally wounded by the same shell. Helmer's death had a profound affect on McCrae, who was moved to write *In Flanders Fields* the following day. The poem was published in Punch Magazine in December 1915.

It has been said that McCrae stared at Helmer's grave in Essex Farm as he wrote the poem. Unfortunately, Helmer has no known grave, but a memorial cross raised to Helmer was found near the bunkers in 1919. No remains were found and how his grave became lost was never established. Today, Helmer is commemorated on the Menin Gate Memorial to the Missing.

McCrae died of pneumonia at Wimereux, France, January 28, 1918 at the age of 45.

To visit the bunkers where McCrae wrote *In Flanders Fields*, follow the signs to Dixmuide north of Ypres. You will see Essex Farm Cemetery on your right about one kilometre down the road. The bunkers are just north of the cemetery, but are in very bad condition. Caution is advised

IN FLANDERS FIELDS

In Flanders fields the poppies blow
Between the crosses, row on row,
    That mark our place; and in the sky
    The larks, still bravely singing, fly
Scarce heard amid the guns below.

We are the Dead. Short days ago
We lived, felt dawn, saw sunset glow,
    Loved, and were loved, and now we lie
    In Flanders fields.

Take up your quarrel with the foe:
To you from failing hands we throw
    The torch; be yours to hold it high.
    If ye break faith with us who die
We shall not sleep, though poppies grow
    In Flanders fields.

HAGUE, OWEN CARSLEY FREDERIC, Lieut., 7th Battery, 2nd Brigade, Canadian Field Artillery, eldest *s.* of Frederic Hague, of Montreal, Advocate, by his wife, Mary, dau. of Samuel Carsley, of Montreal ; *b.* Montreal, 23 Feb.

1889 ; educ. High School, Montreal, and McGill University, where he took the degree of B.Sc. in 1909, and M.Sc. in 1914. He was an electrical engineer, and practiced his profession in Montreal. He joined the 2nd Brigade, Field Artillery, in 1912, and with the rest of that Brigade volunteered for active service as soon as the first Canadian Contingent was formed, going to the Front with the 7th Battery. His brigade took part in the severe fighting in April and May, 1915, near Ypres. It was on 2 May he was killed. On the morning of that day he was near his battery on the bank of the Yser 'Canal, St. Julien, with Lieut. Helmer, of Ottawa, when a German heavy shell burst near them. Lieut. Helmer was killed instantly, and Lieut. Hague died that evening. He was buried at Hazebrouck ; *unm.* Col. J. J. Creelman, commanding the 2nd Brigade, wrote as follows : " It is with extreme regret that I write with regard to the death of your son, and let me express my sincere sympathy with you in your great loss. Between 22 and 28 April, when I went into hospital, Owen had done really wonderful work as Section Commander and Forward Observing Officer. His work was splendid, and he showed an absolute disregard of personal safety at those times when his duties required that he expose himself. When in hospital at Rouen I took occasion to write to General Burstall calling attention officially to your son's excellent services and marked bravery during the first six days of the fight at Ypres."

Owen Carsley F. Hague.

From the Roll of Honour

The Medals of John Gloag

MEMORIALS
Mementos of a Life Lost

For many grieving Canadian families, old wounds were opened when the Canadian government memorialized the fallen in the early 1920s.

Through the post, over a period of two years, government mementos arrived in registered envelopes. The first to arrive were the medals, awarded posthumously, engraved with name, service number, rank and unit. A year or so later came the Canadian Memorial or Widow's Cross and often the Next-of-Kin Memorial Plaque or Dead Man's Penny. Each memento was accompanied by papers expecting to be returned in acknowledgment of receipt and expressing kind regards as only mass production can achieve: "grateful people," "brave life," "passed out of the sight of men," "regrets of the Militia Council"; or "he so bravely won." For those whose sons had been dead for six or seven years, the shock of these arrivals must have been difficult.

The items in the photo were sent to the family of Private John Gloag of Winnipeg. An original member of the 8th Canadian Infantry — Little Black Devils — Gloag arrived in France in February 1915. He was killed in action when the 8th retreated to the Gravenstafel Ridge on April 25, 1915 and his body was never found. He was 19.

The Next-of-Kin Plaque or Dead Man's Penny was issued to the families of all British Commonwealth soldiers who died in The Great War. Twelve centimetres in diameter, the bronze casting was designed by E. Carter Preston. More than 1.1 million of the individually-named plaques were issued, about 500 to women.

The 1914-15 Star was awarded to all soldiers serving in an active theatre of war from November 22, 1914 to December 31, 1915. More than 70,000 bronze Stars were awarded to Canadians, each with the name on the reverse.

The British War Medal was similarly awarded to any soldier who served overseas. This silver medal, its edge impressed with the name, service number, rank and unit of the soldier, was awarded to more than 420,000 Canadians. As with all the medals, they were awarded posthumously.

The bronze Victory Medal was awarded for service in an active theater of war and always accompanied the British War Medal. It was named similarly to the British War Medal and was issued to more than 370,000 Canadians.

Unique to Canada was the silver Canadian Memorial Cross or Mother's Cross awarded by the Canadian Government to mothers and wives of fallen Canadians. If the dead serviceman's wife and mother were alive, two crosses were awarded. If both were deceased, then no crosses were awarded. Roughly 60,000 crosses were dispatched, each named on the reverse.

In the Second World War, a similar cross was issued to mothers and widows under the same conditions as in The Great War. The cipher was changed from GVI for George V to GVIR for George VI. New Zealand issued Memorial Crosses in the Second World War, with the fern leaf replacing the maple leaf. The cross was worn as a pendant.

THE ODDS

A shocking statistic of The Great War was the tremendous loss incurred within a few hours of an attack being launched. Suffering 60 to 70 per cent casualties was typical for an attacking battalion of 650. Of every five, one would die and two would be wounded.

Of the 418,000 Canadians who served overseas during the war, 60,000 died. One in seven. However, the 418,000 is not a true reflection as it includes men who never served in France or Flanders and men in such units as the Army Service Corps, the Cavalry, the Siege Artillery, Lines of Communication and Forestry who rarely came under enemy fire.

For an average soldier serving in a front line battalion, such as the 16th, the chance of being killed was one in four. Two out of four were wounded, and only one in four came through the war unscathed. Overall, the odds of dying of wounds were one in ten, but it depended on the location of the wound.

The number of Canadian soldiers wounded in the war was 144,506. Most of the wounds resulted from shellfire.

In many battles, such as Passchendaele, difficult and dangerous conditions prevented removal of the wounded, who succumbed to their wounds. In the later battles of 1918, the medical arrangements and transport system worked like a well-oiled machine and the wounded were evacuated from, say, Cambrai to Rouen or Boulogne within hours.

The toll of the wounded is sad reading:[4]

Head and neck	22,284
Chest	3,780
Abdomen	1,395
Pelvis	53
Upper Extremities	51,508
Lower Extremities	43,652
Suffered ill effects of gas	11,356
Wounded who remained on duty	7,602
Wounded accidentally	2,247
Wounds self-inflicted	729

Amputations:

One leg	1,675
One arm	667
One foot	232
One hand	141
Both legs	47
Both feet	11
Both arms	6
Both legs and both arms	1

---

[4] My grandfather, Private Randall Christie of the 8th Canadian Field Ambulance, was one of the 22,284 soldiers who suffered head and neck wounds. He was playing cards near Mericourt in December 1917. A shrapnel shell exploded and my grandfather received a shrapnel ball in the cheek. He recovered in England, but for him, the war was over. My great-uncle, Lieutenant John Christie, MC, of the Princess Patricia's Canadian Light Infantry, was one of the 43,652 who received wounds to the lower extremities. In my great-uncle's case, he was shot in the knee at Parvillers in August 1918.

Badge commemorating the Canadians at Ypres, 1915

FOR FURTHER REFERENCE

I have outlined below several books that will greatly increase the appreciation and understanding of the immortal salient:

Before Endeavours Fade by R. E. Coombs (the best guide book on the Western Front). Battle of Britain Prints, 6th edition, 1990.

Ypres, Then and Now by J. Giles. Leo Cooper Ltd., 1970.

Ypres and the Battles for Ypres 1914-18, Michelin Guide. Michelin, 1920.

The Ypres Salient by M. Scott (the cemeteries of the salient). Gliddon Books, 1992.

Canada in Flanders Volume I and II by Lord Beaverbook (the Canadians at Ypres 1915 and 1916). Hodder and Stoughton, 1916, 1917.

Death of an Army by A. Farrar-Hockley (on the 1st Battle of Ypres 1914). William Morrow & Co., 1968.

They called it Passchendaele by L. MacDonald (personal reminiscences of the Third Battle of Ypres 1917). MacMillan, 1978.

Legacy of Valour by D. Dancocks (the Canadians at Passchendaele 1917). Hurtig, 1986.

BOOKS ABOUT THE SECOND BATTLE OF YPRES

Welcome to Flanders Fields, by D. Dancocks, McClelland and Stewart, 1988.

Beyond Courage by G. Cassar. Oberon Press, 1985.

History of the Canadian Forces 1914-19 Volume I + Appendices by A. F. Duguid. The Ministry of National Defence, 1938.

The Official History of the Canadian Expeditionary Force 1914-19 by G. W. L. Nicholson. The Queen's Printer, 1962.

Tapestry of War by S. Gwynn. Harper Collins, 1992.

IF YOU SEE THESE
BEFORE YOU'RE MARRIED,
WELL, YOU ARE A
NAUGHTY BOY!

Contemporary First World War Postcard

Tour Map

The Canadians
in the Second Battle
of Ypres
(April 1915)

(Simplified Trench Systems)

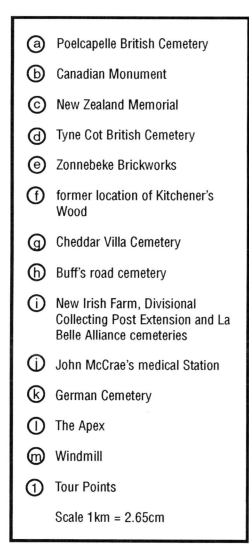

ⓐ Poelcapelle British Cemetery

ⓑ Canadian Monument

ⓒ New Zealand Memorial

ⓓ Tyne Cot British Cemetery

ⓔ Zonnebeke Brickworks

ⓕ former location of Kitchener's Wood

ⓖ Cheddar Villa Cemetery

ⓗ Buff's road cemetery

ⓘ New Irish Farm, Divisional Collecting Post Extension and La Belle Alliance cemeteries

ⓙ John McCrae's medical Station

ⓚ German Cemetery

ⓛ The Apex

ⓜ Windmill

① Tour Points

Scale 1km = 2.65cm

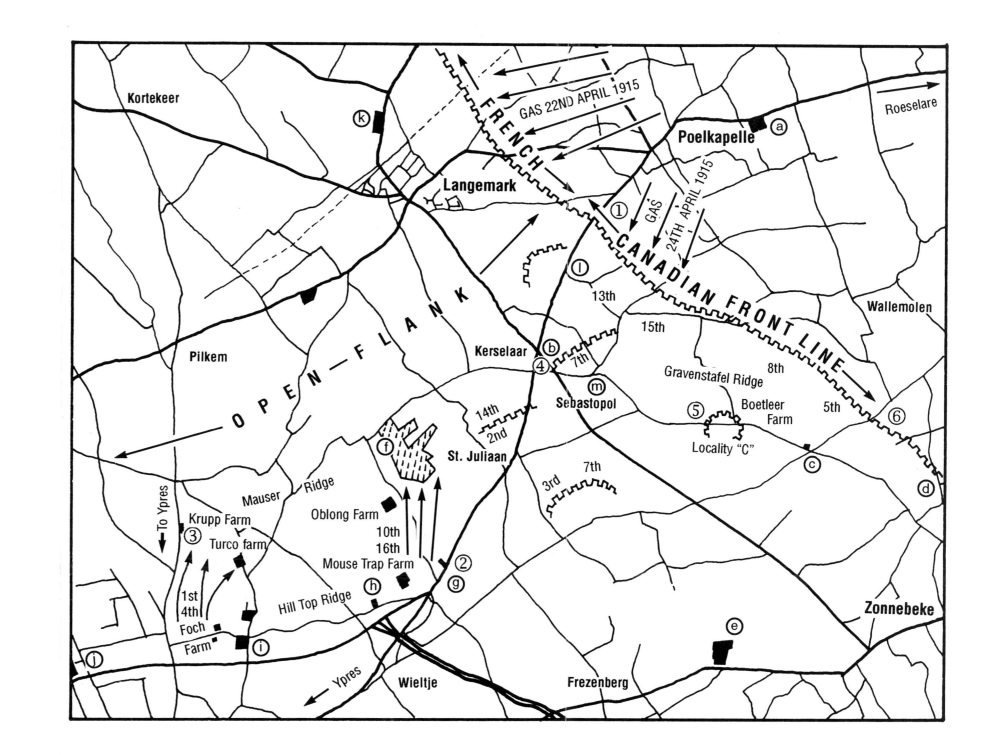